UNSHAKEABLE FAITH

8 TRAITS *for* ROCK-SOLID LIVING

KATHY HOWARD

NEW HOPE
PUBLISHERS
Birmingham, Alabama

New Hope® Publishers
P. O. Box 12065
Birmingham, AL 35202-2065
www.newhopepublishers.com
New Hope Publishers is a division of WMU®.

Library of Congress Cataloging-in-Publication Data Howard, Kathy, 1961-
    Unshakeable faith : 8 traits for rock-solid living / Kathy Howard.
        p. cm.
    ISBN 978-1-59669-297-8 (sc)
    1. Christian women--Religious life. 2. Peter, the Apostle, Saint. 3. Faith.
I. Title.

    BV4527.H72 2011
    248.8'43--dc22

                                2010034775

ISBN-10: 1-59669-297-9
ISBN-13: 978-1-59669-297-8

N114134• 0211 • 4M1

Other New Hope Books
by Kathy Howard

*Before His Throne: Discovering the Wonder of Intimacy
with a Holy God*

*God's Truth Revealed: Biblical Foundations
for the Christian Faith*

TABLE OF CONTENTS

Acknowledgments

Two groups of amazing women significantly contributed to this study. First, I want to thank the strong, brave women who allowed me to share their hearts with you: Karen, Janet, Tonya, Dana, Wende, Julie, Lauren, and Lisa. My prayer is that their faith stories will inspire you to stand firm when life's circumstances are shaky. Second, my deepest gratitude goes to my study sisters at Fannin Terrace Baptist Church in Midland, Texas. They willingly and joyfully test drove this study to help make it the best it could be. You girls are a blessing!

INTRODUCTION

Women are usually prepared for anything and everything. We have dozens of recipes for ground meat when money is tight. We carry everything from safety pins to tiny sewing kits in our purses to tighten loose buttons. Those of us who travel with children pack take-along snacks in case they get hungry and extra clothes for when they happen to fall in a puddle. We keep ourselves—and our families—together and running smoothly.

Is our faith as prepared to withstand hard times? Difficulties and trials bombard us constantly. Everything, from the normal stresses of daily life to the grief of loss, threatens to shake our faith, leaving us and those we love resembling a pile of rubble. But an unshakeable faith will keep us standing firm through all the storms of life.

We can learn a lot about unshakeable faith from the Apostle Peter. I've always been partial to Peter. I think it's because I feel I'm like him in many ways. Peter was simply an ordinary person, a fisherman. He worked hard. He had a family and friends. Peter was passionate and a natural leader, but he was also headstrong and impetuous.

Jesus called this ordinary person for an extraordinary purpose. Simon the fisherman would become Peter the Rock. This outspoken Galilean would lead Christ's church, stand strong in the face of persecution, and even refuse to waver when faced with death. How could this be?

On the night Jesus was betrayed, Peter impulsively declared he would go with Jesus to prison and even death. Yet only hours later, he fled the garden of Gethsemane and fearfully denied even knowing Jesus. But then 30 years and many experiences after that, during Nero's horrid persecution of Christians in Rome, Peter boldly died for his faith in Christ. What made the difference?

Over the next eight sessions we will examine eight "faith traits" God instilled in this unstable believer. These traits would produce an unshakeable faith that would weather every storm Peter encountered. We will walk with Peter as he walked with

Jesus. We will learn what Peter learned. Our goal is to allow God to do in our lives what He did in Peter's life.

These eight faith traits are spiritual characteristics that demonstrate we have an obedient, dependent, and trusting relationship with our Savior. This study can help you build an unshakeable, rock-solid faith that you can stand on when difficulty comes.

Each session focuses on one faith trait and includes the following:

LEARNING IT—From the Gospels and the Book of Acts, we will explore moments Peter had with Jesus that God used to develop the faith trait.

TEACHING IT—From Acts, 1 Peter, and 2 Peter, we will reflect on portions of Peter's teaching on that trait.

LIVING IT—Then we will examine our own lives, to actively apply the biblical truths we learned.

Each session ends with a "Faith Shaker," a story about a real woman living her faith in the midst of a difficult circumstance. Our faith can grow by the testimony of how God worked in others' lives.

Don't miss the journal pages at the end of the book. I've learned in my own spiritual journey that writing about what God teaches me helps reinforce the lessons in my heart and mind.

You can complete the entire session in one sitting or do a section a day for three days. The material is equally effective for group or individual study.

I am excited and honored to share this journey with you. Let's get started.

Week One

He Picked Me!

But you are a chosen people, a royal priesthood, a holy nation, God's special possession, that you may declare the praises of him who called you out of darkness into his wonderful light.

—1 Peter 2:9

*I*t had been a bad day. Nothing really big, just a whole lot of little things. I had complained to God and one of my close friends, but I was pretty determined to be in a bad mood. I only had one more errand before I could go home and wallow in self-pity for the rest of the evening. Since I only needed a handful of things from Walmart—milk, toilet paper, and fabric dye—I expected to be in and out in just a few minutes.

Storming around the store with my "poor me" attitude, I found the fabric dye on the aisle with the laundry detergent. Dark brown was only available in the liquid version. I needed a lot, so I started pulling bottles off the little shelf over my head. Each time I grabbed one, the others were pushed forward by a spring-loaded mechanism on the shelf.

As I lifted the next to last bottle, the one behind it shot out and up. There was no time to take cover, it all happened too fast. When the bottle hit the tile floor, the cap popped off, and dark liquid squirted across the aisle splattering everything in its path, including me. As I surveyed the damage, God spoke to me quietly. *"OK, you've been whining all day. How are you going to respond to this?"*

While I sponged myself off with the paper towels hung on a nearby post, I considered my options. I could continue down the path I'd been on all day and let this dark mess be the last straw that pushed me over the edge to a full-blown, self-absorbed tantrum. Or, I could remember that God is in control. He not only is aware of all the problems, issues, and worries in my life, He cares about each one.

In that moment of decision, God brought a Scripture passage to mind; *"Come to me, all you who are weary and burdened, and I will give you rest"* (Matthew 11:28). Rest in Jesus or throw a fit on the detergent aisle in Walmart? This time I chose Jesus. And I pray I will next time too.

Life is full of trials, both big and small. Most days, the troubles are nothing more than a messy nuisance. Sometimes, though, they aren't so easy to clean up. As women, we are the rescuers, the nurturers, the ones that keep everything together and running smoothly for our families and friends. But can we stand strong—for ourselves and the ones who depend on us—when the truly hard times come?

A rock-solid faith in the one true God provides a firm foundation that is not easily moved. The life of the Apostle Peter reveals how God can grow a fragile faith into a strong, unshakeable faith. Over the next eight sessions, we will explore the life and teachings of Peter, to discover eight "faith traits" God developed in his life and to seek to apply them to our own.

In week one, we will witness Jesus choosing Peter to follow Him as a disciple. If you are a Christian—if you have entered into a saving relationship with Jesus Christ—it's because God chose you first. Have you ever taken a moment to dwell on the incredible truth that God chose you? As we study Peter's teaching, you will discover the great significance of being chosen and the difference it should make in your life that Jesus chose you.

Unshakeable Faith Trait One
Secure in the God Who Loves and Chooses You

Learning It
Many people gathered around Jesus during His earthly ministry, but Jesus specifically chose 12 men to follow Him. Jesus taught, trained, and prepared these men to carry on His purposes after He was gone. All four Gospels record Jesus calling His disciples. John's

Unshakeable Faith

account may be Jesus' initial encounter with Peter, while Matthew, Mark, and Luke each report a variation on a later event.

Read John 1:35–42. **Describe how Peter met Jesus.**

⫸ Describe the time you first met Jesus. Who made the introductions?

What was your initial impression of Jesus? Did you accept Him as Lord and Savior right away or did it take time?

Reread John 1:42. **What did Jesus say to Peter when they met?**

The first time they met, Jesus gave Peter a new name. Today that seems extremely odd. However, in ancient Jewish culture, names were significant. They revealed character or represented a specific purpose God had for that person. The Simon that Jesus met was brash, outspoken, and a bit unstable. The name *Peter* (or Cephas as in some translations) means "rock."

This young man named Simon, who would become Peter, was impetuous, impulsive, and overeager. He needed to become like a rock, so that is what Jesus named him. Jesus changed Simon's name, it appears, because He wanted the nickname to be a perpetual reminder to him about who he should be.

John MacArthur
Twelve Ordinary Men

⊰◁ Considering Simon's personality, why do you think Jesus called him Peter or Rock?

Jesus did not completely replace Simon with Peter. Throughout the Gospels, Jesus occasionally called Peter by his old name, Simon. This usually happened when Peter acted in a way that did not reflect his new name, Rock. Jesus used the name Simon as a rebuke, to remind Peter to leave the old character behind. Jesus had a plan and purpose for Peter. To fulfill his purpose, he needed to be Peter, not Simon. From the time they met, Jesus worked in Peter's heart and life, shaping and molding him into the man He could use.

The passage in John does not tell us that Peter left his fishing business to follow Jesus at that point. But Jesus made it clear He had plans for Peter by giving him a new name. Now, let's take a look at what might have been Peter's next significant encounter with Jesus.

Read Luke 5:1–11. **What was Jesus doing on the shore of the lake? Why did He need Simon Peter's boat?**

When Jesus came along, Peter and his fishing partners were washing their nets and preparing to go home. They had fished all night without success. Yet, when Jesus finished teaching the crowd, He told Peter to take the boat back out into the water and put the freshly cleaned nets down for a catch.

How did Simon respond? How do you think he felt about the direction? What was the result?

↳ Think of a time when God guided you in a direction that did not seem logical to you. Did you obey? How did God work in this situation?

↳ Why do you think Jesus performed this particular miracle in Peter's life? What change did it bring about in Simon Peter?

Jesus never does anything halfway! The catch was so large they had to call for another boat. But the large catch of fish was not the only miracle that day; Peter's perception of Jesus changed. Therefore, Peter's perception of himself changed. When Peter recognized the power and authority of Jesus, he also humbly became aware of his own sin. Now Peter was ready to follow Jesus.

> This sea-incident represented a major crisis in Peter's experience, for the miraculous catch of fish brought the fisherman to realize that the One who had commanded him to cast his net was no mere man, but the Master of ocean, and earth, and sky. Henceforth Jesus became his Lord.
>
> Herbert Lockyer
> *All the Apostles of the Bible*

Peter's *"obedience"* in verse 5 seems more like appeasement than action based on belief in Jesus. But Peter went from tired fisherman one minute to eager follower the next. What made the difference?

Jesus had a plan and purpose for Peter before they even met. Jesus changed his name from Simon to Peter to reflect the character Jesus would develop in him. Jesus knew that Peter would have to face many trials and intense persecution. Peter needed a rock-solid faith that would not be shaken when the hard times came.

Here on the lake, Peter recognized that he had been chosen by one with authority. It was enough to make him leave everything behind. But it was only the beginning of his faith journey.

TEACHING IT

As Peter followed Jesus, he learned more about the significance of being chosen by God. What Peter learned, he passed on to those he taught. After Jesus' resurrection and ascension, Peter became one of the primary leaders in the Jerusalem church. We also know from biblical evidence and church tradition that Peter traveled, visiting churches and spreading the gospel, before he was martyred in Rome under Emperor Nero in the late A.D. 60s.

First and 2 Peter were probably written from Rome during the latter years of Peter's life.

Read 1 Peter 1:1–5. **Depending on your translation, you will see the words** *elect, chosen,* **or both used to describe the recipients of Peter's letter. Considering this description, who took the initiative in the salvation of the "elect"? Was it Peter's audience or God?**

⇥ What does this truth mean in regard to your own salvation?

All three persons of the Trinity actively participate in salvation as verse two reveals. We are chosen by God the Father; our salvation is made possible by the sacrificial blood of Jesus the Son; and we move from spiritual death to life through the sanctifying presence of the Holy Spirit. That's a miracle only God can perform!

How did Peter respond to God's salvation in verse 3?

Read verses 3 and 4 from the NIV below. **Circle all the words Peter used that describe our glorious salvation.**

"Praise be to the God and Father of our Lord Jesus Christ! In his great mercy he has given us new birth into a living hope through the resurrection of Jesus Christ from the dead, and into an inheritance that can never perish, spoil or fade—kept in heaven for you" (1 Peter 1:3–4).

✎ Describe this great gift of salvation in your own words.

Now read 1 Peter 2:9-10. **List the four phrases used in verse 9 to describe believers.**

Peter also used some "before and after" language in these same verses to describe salvation. Read the "before" phrases below on the left and complete them with the correct "after" description.

BEFORE	AFTER
Darkness	
Not a people	
Not received mercy	

According to the second half of verse 9, how does God intend for believers to respond to this glorious "choosing?"

LIVING IT

I have been friends with Janet for more than 20 years. We met in church in Casper, Wyoming where both of our husbands had been transferred with their oil industry jobs. After our initial meeting, Janet began to call me to chat and invite me to lunch. Our friendship developed quickly and even though we have both moved several times over the years we've remained close. I'll never forget something Janet told me a little while after our friendship was forged. "The first time I met you I decided I wanted you to be my friend. I picked you out." She chose me. And I am so glad.

⤷ Think back to a time when you were chosen. For a job. As a spouse. To be a leader. To be a friend. How did you feel about being chosen?

Read Ephesians 1:4–5 from the New Living Translation below.

"Even before he made the world, God loved us and chose us in Christ to be holy and without fault in his eyes. God decided in advance to adopt us into his own family by bringing us to himself through Jesus Christ ... and it gave him great pleasure" (Ephesians 1:4–5 NLT).

Circle the words in the passage above that describe God's action on your behalf.

How did God feel about doing this for you?

How does it feel to be chosen by God for salvation and adopted into His family?

According to Ephesians 1:4–5, how should you respond to this "choosing"?

Believer, God chose you before the creation of the world. He picked you out for His very own, before you were even born. All of us were once spiritually dead because of our sin, but while we were still sinners, Jesus paid the penalty for our sin through His death on the Cross. And in His great mercy, God gave us new birth into a living hope through the resurrection of Jesus from the dead.

Read "Faith Shaker" and then answer the questions that follow.

FAITH SHAKER

Bill physically left Karen the day before their 25th wedding anniversary, but he had been in the process of leaving for a long time. He had started to drift away about five years earlier. He pursued interests on his own, resented the demands of family life, and even denied the God he had once believed in. Karen did everything she could think of to draw her husband back, but all her attempts seemed to push him further away.

Karen felt like she had lost her husband long before Bill admitted he wanted out of their marriage. His long disengagement had made her feel ignored, devalued, and ugly. His final act of walking out the door told Karen she was unwanted and unlovable. "The one person who promised to love me forever said he didn't anymore."

Karen begged God to fix everything—to fix Bill, to fix their marriage, to fix her. Many times she poured out her anger and distress while meeting with God on the floor of her dark closet. But the divorce still happened. So Karen clung to God.

"God did not save my marriage, but He did save me. He faithfully cared for me. Like when His people showed up to serve me, listen to me, or sit with me while I cried. And when the money I needed was there, and the lawn was mowed, and the children were loved on."

After three years and a lot of prayer, godly counsel, and Bible study, Karen knows she is dearly loved and wanted by God. "I was told that if I let Him, God would fill my every need as a single woman—my need to feel safe, secure, and loved. I did not fully believe that when I heard it, but God has certainly done it."

What new things did Karen learn about God and how were they confirmed through her experience with Him?

How did these things directly meet her most urgent need?

The fact that God chose you and loves you can sustain you through the difficult periods of your life. Write how this truth applies to the possible situations below:

- When you've been rejected by others

- When you feel alone

- When you have experienced failure

- Other

What situation are you facing right now in which you need to remember that God loves you and has chosen you?

Sweet sister in Christ, God loves you and chose you to be His very own. As we end this session, take some time to consider this amazing, eternal truth. Write a prayer below to express your gratefulness to God.

Week Two

It's Who You Know

"Therefore, let all Israel be assured of this: God has made this Jesus, whom you crucified, both Lord and Messiah."

—Acts 2:36

*I*t hit without warning. Halfway up the mountain the wind began to howl. By the time my husband, our two young daughters, and I got off the chair lift at the top of the ridge, visibility was less than three feet due to the blowing snow.  I couldn't even see my ski boots. Kelley, who was about 11 at the time, was crying hysterically. And 8-year-old Sarah had both her legs and arms wrapped around me with her head buried in my belly.

Wayne and I hollered at each other over the screaming wind and the screaming child. We had never been to the Lake Louise Ski Resort before and didn't know the trails. In fact, we couldn't even *see* the trails. And it was difficult just to keep our heads up because ice blasted any exposed skin.

We tried to get the girls moving—we had to get out of the storm—but neither of them would budge. Just when *I* was about to start crying, a masked skier approached our family.

"My name is Luke. I see you're in trouble. I'm a member of the ski patrol and know these trails like the back of my hand. I'd like to help you get down if that's all right."

That was more than all right. It was an answer to prayer.

Kelley calmed down when she heard Luke's qualifications and his offer to help. She got right behind him and held on to his jacket. I got close behind her with Sarah's skis between mine and Wayne brought up the rear to make sure we didn't lose anyone. Within minutes Luke had led us far enough down the mountain to get below the whiteout. Then he was gone.

Kelley and Sarah had refused to follow Wayne and me because we didn't know the way. Plus they probably sensed our own fear. They were young, but not dumb. However, Luke was different. He not only claimed to know the way, he had the strength and authority to make us believe him. That gave the girls the confidence they needed to follow him.

Do you have confidence in the One you follow? Are you secure in the Person you call Lord? In week two, we'll examine the identity of Jesus. We'll see how Peter's growing understanding of the nature of Jesus strengthened his faith and gave him the confidence to follow Him no matter where He led.

UNSHAKEABLE FAITH TRAIT TWO

Confident in Your All-Powerful, All-Knowing, Sovereign God

LEARNING IT

In week one we studied Peter's call to follow Jesus. When Peter left his nets and joined the ranks of the Twelve, he knew Jesus was a great teacher sent by God, but he still had much to learn about Him. As the weeks and months passed, Peter and the others became eyewitnesses to the power and authority of Jesus.

⊰ Look up the following Scriptures. Each passage relates a miracle of Jesus that demonstrates His divine authority over a specific area. Draw lines from the passages on the left to the corresponding areas of power and authority on the right. (Note: Many biblical scholars believe that Mark based his Gospel record on Peter's eyewitness testimony.)

Mark 1:21–28	nature
Mark 1:40–42	demons
Mark 2:1–11	material world
Mark 4:35–41	disease
Mark 5:35–43	forgiveness of sin
Mark 6:39–44	death

Now, consider the power of God that Peter witnessed in Jesus. Does God have power to work in the circumstances of your life? (Check one.)

___ Yes.

___ I'm not sure.

___ I know He does, but I'm afraid He won't work the way I want Him to work.

Jesus' popularity grew because of the miracles. Massive crowds gathered everywhere He and the disciples went. Many came because they had physical needs, but they were also amazed with His teaching because *"He taught as one who had authority"* (Matthew 7:28–29). However, Jesus said some things the people did not find very appealing.

Read John 6:26–40. **What did Jesus offer the people in this passage that He alone has the power and authority to give?**

Once again the crowds had found Jesus. Even after all they'd already seen they demanded Jesus perform a miraculous sign as proof He had been sent from God (6:30). Jesus knew that no sign would convince them. Belief would require the Father's activity in their hearts (6:44). Jesus did not give them what they wanted, but He offered what they needed—Himself. Eternal life, security, fulfillment, and more were all available in Jesus. However, His declaration about being the Bread of life fell on hard hearts.

Read John 6:60–69. **How did many respond to this "hard teaching" of Jesus? According to verse 65, why did they respond this way?**

✒ What did Jesus ask the Twelve? How did Peter respond?

Why do you think Peter responded so differently than the "many"?

I love Peter's declaration. He had decided to stand firm in the knowledge that Jesus is *"the Holy One of God"* even if things got hard. I have prayed similar words during times of difficulty and doubt. Times when I'm not sure what God is doing. Times when even for a brief moment I want to throw in the towel and do something else. *But, Lord, where else would I go? Only You have the words of life.*

All our lives long we might talk of Jesus, and yet we should never come to an end of the sweet things that might be said of Him. Eternity will not be long enough to learn all He is, or to praise Him for all He has done, but then, that matters not; for we shall be always with Him, and we desire nothing more.

A. W. Tozer,
The Pursuit of God:
A 31-Day Experience

Now read Matthew 16:13–17. **What truth about Jesus was Peter certain of? How did Peter come to know this when others did not?**

What does this teach us about how our own understanding of God is increased?

As we will learn in the next session, Peter's knowledge about Jesus did not keep him from sometimes still trusting in himself—leaning on his own understanding. However, this truth was a solid foundation on which God planned to build an unshakeable faith. In fact, just six days later, God granted to Peter, James, and John the tremendous blessing of seeing the unveiled glory of Christ.

✑ *Read Matthew 17:1–9.* **What was significant about this event?**

Why do you think only this "inner circle" of disciples got to witness it?

Peter, not sure how to act in this situation, impulsively suggested building three shelters. How did God the Father rebuke Peter, yet also increase his understanding?

Not long after this event Jesus turned toward Jerusalem to fulfill the Father's will. These future leaders and witnesses of the Christian faith needed to experience the glory of Christ to stand firm in the days ahead.

TEACHING IT

Assurance in the identity of Christ gave Peter confidence to proclaim Him boldly and follow Him even when things got tough. Let's take a look at Peter's very first sermon to observe the effect. On the day of Pentecost, Peter and the other disciples received the gift Jesus had promised—the indwelling of the Holy Spirit. Filled with the Spirit and armed with the truth, Peter spoke to the thousands gathered in Jerusalem.

Read Acts 2:22–24 and 36. **List all the facts Peter gave about Jesus.**

By whose will and for whose purpose was Jesus crucified? (Circle one.)

God   the Jews

⇥ Why is this truth important?

What did Peter want to make absolutely sure his audience understood? (See v. 36.)

This was not mere head knowledge for Peter. The identity and work of Jesus Christ saturated everything Peter said and did. For example, in the third chapter of Acts, we read about Peter and John healing a crippled man in the name of Jesus. (We'll study this closer in week five.) While he had the attention of the onlookers, Peter urged them to turn to Jesus for salvation. Peter and John were then jailed by the Jewish leaders for teaching about the resurrection of Jesus. The next day they were brought before the ruling council.

Read Acts 4:8–13. **What declaration did Peter make in verse 12?**

From what you've learned so far in this study, did Peter have evidence to back up this kind of absolute statement? If so, what was it?

⊰⊱ How did Peter's complete confidence in the Person of Christ have an impact on his life?

Over three decades later, the identity of Christ was still the driving force of Peter's life. Written near the end of his life, the letter we call 2 Peter is a permanent record of the indelible mark Jesus made on the apostle.

Read **2 Peter 1:16–18. What event — that Peter personally witnessed — did he refer to here?**

⊰⊱ Write a description below of the Jesus Peter knew.

Why was Peter so absolutely certain about the identity and authority of Jesus?

God Can

If God is able to do anything, then why do His children still face illness, grief, and pain? There is no easy answer. However, there are basic principles in Scripture that will help us understand.

God is all-powerful and in control of every situation.
    Psalm 77:14; Jeremiah 32:17; Ephesians 1:18–21

God knows and cares about every aspect of our lives.
    Matthew 6:25–34; Hebrews 4:15; Philippians 4:19

God is good, loving, and faithful.
    Psalm 145:17; 1 John 4:8; Lamentations 3:22–23

We are not alone in our trials; God is always with us.
    Isaiah 43:2; Psalm 23:4; John 14:16; Matthew 28:20

God will strengthen and comfort us in the midst of troubles.
    Psalm 147:3; Isaiah 40:27–31; 2 Corinthians 1:3–4;
    Philippians 4:13

God works through difficulties in our lives to accomplish His eternal purposes.
    James 1:2–4; Romans 5:3–5; 1 Peter 1:6–7; Romans 8:28–29

Living It

Each day we sort of drag ourselves out of bed, get ourselves or the kids off to school, spend hours at work, do laundry, cook dinner, clean toilets, tackle homework, then fall into bed—only to get up and do it all over again. Does the identity of Jesus truly matter in the midst of this, our daily lives?

Let's see what God's Word says about the Person and work of Jesus Christ. Read the following passages and fill out the table below.

PASSAGE	WORD/ PHRASE THAT TEACHES JESUS IS GOD	OTHER TRUTHS ABOUT JESUS AND HOW HE WORKS IN US
2 Corinthians 4:4–6		
Colossians 2:9–10		
1 Timothy 1:15–17		
Titus 2:11–14		

⊰⊱ Based on what you've learned in this session, write a description below of the Person of Jesus Christ. Include who He is, what authority He has, and what He has accomplished.

Has your view of Jesus been limited? Has it been expanded today through these Scriptures? If so, in what ways?

⊰ Now think about the tasks and people that fill your life. Prayerfully consider how these truths about Jesus can and should make a difference as you do your work and relate to others. Record whatever God tells you below.

In addition to the usual struggles of everyday life, sometimes we face harder, more consuming trials. Remembering who God is can mean the difference between standing firm and being swept away.

Read "Faith Shaker" and then answer the questions that follow.

FAITH SHAKER

Janet has clung to the sovereignty of our all-powerful God since the day she received the diagnosis. There are treatments, but no cure, for myelofibrosis. This rare bone marrow disorder disrupts the normal production of blood cells. Extensive scarring in the bone marrow leads to severe anemia, weakness, fatigue, and often, an enlarged spleen and liver.

Janet's treatment began with regular injections of human growth hormone intended to increase her red blood cell count. In the midst of this physical trial, she felt spiritually strong. An entry from Janet's journal reads, "God has continued to be my strength. He encourages me through Scripture, answered prayer, songs, and friends and family."

After three months of injections, the count did not improve. So, the doctors chose a different course—an infusion of a chemotherapy drug every three weeks. This particular drug, regularly used to treat metastasized cancer, is only used for myelofibrosis in a clinical trial. Janet is one of only eight patients in the United States on this treatment protocol.

Through this uncertainty, God reminded Janet who He is. Another journal entry reads, "I am more and more mindful that God is huge! He knows the stars, and He knows the number of our days! I trust Him to be huge in the midst of things that are uncontrollable."

Now, more than a year later, Janet's battle with myelofibrosis continues. Some days she is exhausted. Sometimes she is discouraged. But she is still leaning on God's character. "While I know that the Lord is the great physician and will do as He chooses—my spirit is weak. But, I remind myself of His great love. God is good—all the time. Feelings ebb and flow, but His power doesn't depend on my feelings. I can trust Him in all situations."

How is Janet's faith helping her during a painful and uncertain time in her life?

Are there any chronic or deteriorating situations in your life right now? If yes, what are they?

What do you want God to do in your situation? Do you believe He can do that?

How can God help you and be your strength if He chooses to work in another way in your situation? Spend a few moments reflecting on the Scriptures and truths found in the sidebar "God Can" on page 32 to help you with your answer.

How will you respond to Him if He chooses to work in another way?

As the Bread of life, Jesus declared He could meet our every need and satisfy our deepest longings. He also claimed to be the only way to God (John 14:6). Peter, who had followed Jesus, saw His glory, and witnessed His death and resurrection, stood firm in these truths for the rest of his life. Will you?

As we end this session, prayerfully reflect on the biblical truths in the "God Can" sidebar on page 32 again. Ask God to show you how these truths about who He is and what He has promised can help you stand firm, even through life's most difficult trials.

*God's Word is clear that salvation is found in Jesus Christ alone. There is no other way to God. Has there been a moment in your life when you placed your faith and trust in Jesus Christ as Savior and Lord? If not, why not do that now. Salvation is found in no one else!

Week Three

Let Yourself Go

*Then Jesus said to his disciples, "Whoever wants to be my disciple
must deny themselves and take up their cross and follow me."*
— Matthew 16:24

Our second daughter, Sarah, could have been the poster
child for Dr. James Dobson's widely read book *The
Strong-Willed Child*. From the womb this precious girl
bucked authority of every
kind. She was determined to
get her own way in every situation.

You may be thinking that I just
didn't know how to handle such a
determined youngster. I thought
that too. So, I bought Dr. Dobson's
book and read it cover to cover. Then
I cried, because I had already been doing everything he suggested
and none of it made an impact.

In her preschool years, I could not simply send Sarah to her
room for a time-out — because she refused to stay there. I had to
stand in the hallway and hold the door closed. In her grade school
years, my husband and I tried every parenting tool and trick
we came across — from encouragement and rewards for good
behavior to restrictions and loss of privileges for disobedience.

When Sarah entered high school, this battle of wills intensi-
fied. It would have been so much easier if we had given up and
let her have her way. But we knew there was a lot more at stake
than merely whether or not Sarah recognized our authority.

Sarah pushed and fought but we continued to stand our
ground. She didn't like us and didn't keep it a secret. Our home
often felt like a war zone. She refused to yield to our experience
and wisdom in so many situations. We knew the ramifications of
her behavior better than she, yet she continued to resist. And we
continued to pray.

Now we know that even though we couldn't see it, God was working in Sarah's heart. She has grown into an amazing young woman who loves the Lord and desires to please Him. She is sensitive to the needs of others and goes out of her way to help. She also loves her family and likes spending time with us!

Now in her second year of college, Sarah is studying early childhood education. She wants to be a kindergarten teacher. How's that for an ironic twist of fate?

Many of you can relate to our parenting experience. It seems ridiculous that a four-year-old child—or a teenager for that matter—will stubbornly insist on their own way. Do they really believe they know better than their wiser, more-experienced parents? Yet, we do the same thing with God. Each of us has been that strong-willed child who refuses to submit to the Father's authority. Sometimes it's from outright rebellion. Sometimes it's simply because we think we know best.

In this session, we will drop in on a couple of occasions when Peter tried to impose his will over the Father's plan. I'm praying we can learn more about submitting to God by studying Peter's example of what not to do. As we'll see, even hard-headed Peter eventually learned that God deserved his yielded obedience.

UNSHAKEABLE FAITH TRAIT THREE

Submitted to the One Who Knows the Future and Has a Plan

LEARNING IT

God had given Peter a supernatural understanding of the identity of Jesus Christ. However, this intellectual knowledge did not always have an impact on Peter's actions. More than once, Peter thought his way was better than Jesus'. In fact, he even tried to impose his will on Jesus. We would never do that, right?

⫸ *Read Matthew 16:21–23.* (This happened not long after Peter's great confession.) Detail the Father's plans for Jesus in the space below.

Notice the two words *must go*, which Jesus included in His details of upcoming events to His disciples. This was not a plan Jesus was toying with, or suggestions from the Father He was considering. The Father had revealed His will and Jesus was determined to submit to that will obediently and completely.

Now, in turn, God in human form revealed these plans to His disciples. Incredible! Jesus unfolded the Father's plan of salvation for the whole world to this group of 12 ordinary men.

How should they have reacted to such a glorious revelation?

How did Peter react instead? Put a check next to the following phrase that most accurately describes Peter's reaction.

___ Yes, Lord! And what do You want me to do?
___ Praise God for providing mercy and grace to sinners like me!
___ Lord, is there some other way?
___ Lord, this is a hard thing to bear. Give me strength and help me to trust in Your plan.
___ No way! We're not doing it like that!

⫸ Now go back and put a star next to the statement that most accurately reflects your usual reaction when God shows you His will.

> Peter's strong will and warm heart linked to his ignorance produce a shocking bit of arrogance. He confesses that Jesus is the Messiah and then speaks in a way implying that he knows more of God's will than the Messiah himself.
>
> D. A. Carson
> *The Expositor's Bible Commentary: Matthew*

Peter likely had good intentions; he wanted to protect Jesus. Although Peter calls Jesus *"Lord,"* the nature of his correction reveals he wasn't yielding to His lordship in that moment. The Greek construction of Peter's statement is extremely strong. It would be like us saying "No way, no how, not ever!"

Jesus quickly responded to Peter's "ignorant arrogance" with an even sharper rebuke. Jesus knew that Satan would try to use Peter's words to tempt him to abandon the Father's will and follow an "easier," less painful path. Not long before this, Peter had made his great confession and Jesus called him a *"rock."* But in this moment, when Peter tries to exert his own will, Jesus calls him a *"stumbling block."*

Jesus revealed the heart of Peter's misguided intentions in verse 23. What was the core issue?

Many of us have the same problem Peter had. We see things with our limited, selfish, human perspective instead of God's eternal, all-knowing perspective. Intellectually, I accept that God knows best and His way is perfect. However, I still want to do things my way, even while knowing from experience that I usually get it wrong. Jesus has a solution for this "ignorant arrogance" that plagued our friend Peter and that still plagues us today.

Read Matthew 16:24–26. List the three things Jesus said a person must do to be His disciple.

꘏ Describe what is at stake. What do we lose by being Jesus' disciple? What do we gain?

Jesus' directive to *"take up your cross"* is often misunderstood to be some great burden we've been given to bear in this life, like a wayward child or a chronic illness. God does sometimes allow these things into our lives for His purposes, but that is not what Jesus meant here. The Cross represented Jesus' complete submission to the Father's will. In this ultimate act of obedience Jesus fulfilled God's plan for His life. To take up our cross, therefore, means to submit ourselves fully to obeying God no matter where He leads.

Sometimes I hesitate in completely obeying God because I don't want to let go of my own dreams and goals. Can you relate? Yet, whatever God has for us is far better than anything we can dream up for ourselves. When we lose our own "dreams" we gain God's *destiny and purpose* for us. What could be better than that?

Even after Jesus' rebuke and lesson on true discipleship, Peter still had trouble letting go of his own dreams for Jesus. Let's go back to the garden of Gethsemane.

Read John 18:1–11. **Describe the scene including Peter's brash action.**

Why do you think Peter responded as he did? You may come up with several reasons.

Based on Jesus' rebuke, what had Peter not yet fully grasped?

Once again, no matter what Peter's intentions, he was not guided by kingdom priorities, but by earthly ones. He still had a lot to learn. (By the way, the Gospel writer Luke tells us that Jesus reversed the damage Peter caused by healing the man's ear!) Let's take a look at one more passage to see that Peter actually did begin to learn that God's way is the right way.

Read Acts 10:23b–29. **(If you are unfamiliar with this story, you may want to read Acts 10:1–29 to understand the context of this passage.)**

A Gentile, a Roman centurion named Cornelius, asked Peter, a Jew, to come to his home. Cornelius and his family wanted to know about Jesus. Because Jews considered Gentiles to be "unclean," their law did not allow them to associate with non-Jews.

How do Peter's behavior and words show us that he was beginning to submit to God's will rather than follow man's wisdom? (Reread vv. 28–29 to help with your answer.)

Peter may have been a slow learner at times, but he did learn. Like Peter, God often has to teach me the same lesson repeatedly before it sinks in. Of course, it would be easier if I were to learn it the first time.

Teaching It

After Jesus' ascension, brash, outspoken Peter became the disciples' courageous spokesman. Last session, we listened in on his very first sermon on the day of Pentecost to see how confidence in Jesus' identity made Peter a bold witness to a crowd of thousands. Now, let's see how learning to submit to God's will had an impact on Peter's ministry and teaching.

Once, in the early days of the church, Peter healed a crippled man in front of the temple (Acts 3:1–10). The miracle gave him and John the opportunity to share the message of Jesus with the amazed crowd. However, the Jewish leaders were highly upset that they were *"teaching the people, proclaiming in Jesus the resurrection of the dead"* (Acts 4:2). So they arrested Peter and John and kept them in prison overnight. The next day they were brought before the Sanhedrin, the Jewish ruling council, to answer for their actions. Our dear, brave Peter took the opportunity to preach another sermon—this time to the Jewish leaders!

Read Acts 4:13–21. **What command did the Sanhedrin give Peter and John?**

Which of the following influenced the Jewish leaders' command? Check all that apply.

____ They couldn't deny that a miracle had occurred.
____ A lot of people had witnessed this miracle done in the name of Jesus.
____ They wanted the people to know the truth.
____ They were determined to keep the name of Jesus from continuing to spread.

How did Peter and John respond?

Note: This verse does not give us the freedom to resist earthly authority any time we choose. In fact, Peter later writes: *"Submit yourselves for the Lord's sake to every authority"* (1 Peter 2:13). This event in Acts 4 teaches us that, if obedience to a human authority would cause us to disobey God's command, we must choose to obey God.

Did you notice the change in our friend Peter? Instead of thinking in human terms or considering his own comfort, he kept God's will and kingdom priorities first. In turn, he taught others what he'd learned. Although the verses you are about to read are part of a larger passage on suffering and trials, Peter stresses that submission to God is at the heart of how we can approach them.

Read 1 Peter 4:1–3.

᠕ Peter taught that one of two things will determine the direction of our life. Fill in the blanks to complete the two possibilities.

Our own evil human _____

The _____ of God

Based on verse 1, which of these determined the course of Jesus' life?

Peter stated that those who live for the will of God are "done with sin." That doesn't mean we won't ever sin, but it does mean our lives won't be ruled by our sinful desires and passions. Choosing our own will over God's will be the exception rather than the rule. Living for God's will rather than our own also means we won't allow the fear of persecution to hinder our obedience. This is why Peter was able to choose obedience to God in the face of possible human punishment.

> Happy are they who give themselves to God! They are delivered from their passions . . . from this countless mass of evils, because placing our will entirely in the hands of God, we want only what God wants, and thus we find his consolation in faith, and consequently hope in the midst of all sufferings.
>
> Francois Fenelon (1651–1715)
> Excerpt from *Devotional Classics*
> edited by Richard J. Foster and James Bryan Smith

Living It

Peter learned he could live unhindered by the fear of man and free from the burden of his own desires when he submitted himself completely to the will of God. I want to live unhindered and free!

How about you? Then, let's see some of what God's Word says about submission.

Read Romans 8:5–14.

→| **Reread verses 5–8.** Paul, the author of Romans, contrasted life following our own natural desires with life lived following the Spirit of God. List the results and characteristics of each lifestyle in the appropriate column below.

Following our sinful nature	Following the Holy Spirit

By making this comparison, what do you think Paul wanted his readers to understand?

In verses 9–11, Paul established a line of logic to help us grasp some great spiritual truths. If we are truly Christians (belong to Christ) our sinful natures don't control us because the Spirit of Christ lives in us. Although our bodies will still die because of sin, our spirits will live because of the presence of Christ. Not only that, although our bodies die, the same power that raised Christ from the dead will raise our bodies!

⫘ Reread Romans 8:12–14. **Paul says we have an obligation to God because He has given us eternal life through the presence and power of the Spirit of Christ within us. What is this obligation?**

Denying our own will and desires is not always an easy thing to do. Believe me, I know. Sometimes I stubbornly want my own way even when I know it's in direct opposition to God's will. In those moments I must actively choose to obey God instead of doing what I want. Many times I obey Him; sometimes I sinfully go my own way.

God deserves our complete obedience. We are not our own. We belong to Him. He chose us and paid for us with the blood of Christ. But, God is not a strict taskmaster. He does not demand our obedience in order to watch us jump through one divine hoop after another. He has a significant purpose and a loving plan for each of us. Everything He brings or allows into our lives, He wants to use for our spiritual transformation and eternal good. (See Romans 8:28–30.) But He asks for our cooperation.

How do we know God's will so we can obey it? Read "Knowing God's Voice." Although God primarily speaks today through the Bible, He uses other methods to confirm and clarify His will. Circle those things in the margin quote. (Note: God will never guide you in a way that contradicts what He has revealed in His Word.)

Knowing God's Voice

With the Scripture as our guide, we know God can speak in unique ways to individuals. His people will hear and recognize His voice. In our time, God primarily speaks by the Holy Spirit through the Bible, prayer, circumstances, and the church. These four means are difficult to separate. God uses prayer and the Bible together. Often circumstances and the church, or other believers, will help confirm what God is saying to you.

Henry T. Blackaby and Claude V. King
Experiencing God

Read "Faith Shaker" and then answer the questions that follow.

FAITH SHAKER

Tonya was happy right where she was. Ten years ago, she and her family had settled in Cochrane, a small town in Alberta, so her husband, Bo, could attend seminary. For a decade they invested their lives and hearts in that place. Tonya had a fulfilling ministry and close friends. She was completely content, with no desire to leave.

But God had different plans. Bo felt God directing him to accept a pastor's position in Georgia. Although it meant returning to their southern roots, Tonya was deeply grieved to end a period of her life marked strongly by God's activity and a sense of purpose.

The first few weeks in Georgia passed quickly. Settling into the new house. Getting the kids in school. Encouraging Bo. The demands of homemaker, mother, and wife consumed her time and thoughts.

Finally, they unpacked the last box. The kids made new friends. Bo adjusted to his new position. But Tonya—she had no job, no ministry, and few friends. There seemed to be nothing for her in this place.

Tonya felt her new life lacked a specific purpose. So she went to God. "I wanted to hear His big plans for me, but I simply heard, 'study My Word.' What? Surely God didn't bring me 2,500 miles for this? I was anticipating a large ministry, but God confirmed I needed to sit still and study!"

Tonya is still working to give up her own ideas completely and embrace God's immediate plans for her. But the more she lets go of self, the more satisfaction she finds in God. "I've found purpose and perspective in the study of His Word. I've also found contentment in ministering to my family. I don't know what God has in store next year or the next, but I want to follow Him each step of the way."

How were God's plans for Tonya in her new home different than what she expected?

What choice did Tonya ultimately make? Check one of the following:

___ She looked for ministry avenues to serve God in the way she had in mind.
___ She grudgingly obeyed God's direction.
___ She let go of her own plans, submitting her will to God's.
___ What was the result in Tonya's life?

Has God ever led you in a direction vastly different than what you wanted or expected? If so, explain.

Is there a specific issue or area of your life you need to submit to God right now? If so, what is it? Why are you hesitating?

List some truths we should remember about God whenever we struggle with submitting to His leading and authority.

Intellectually, we know that God's way is best. Not only is He worthy of our obedience, but also He knows everything! Who better to call the shots for our future than the One who already knows it?

As we close this session, write a prayer below submitting every area of your life to God. If you're having trouble, ask Him to help you give yourself completely to Him.

Week Four

Don't Forget to Lock Up

"Watch and pray so that you will not fall into temptation. The spirit is willing, but the flesh is weak."

—Mark 14:38

*A*few years ago, in the produce section of the local Super Target, my purse was stolen while I was selecting fruit. Wait, let me clarify. My purse was accidentally stolen. I had turned my back on the cart —containing my purse and other groceries—and stepped a few feet away to the stack of Red Delicious apples. I only took my eyes off the cart for a moment but when I turned back it was gone.

I had no idea what to do; I just stood there looking around. Then I noticed two things. First, an unattended cart—not mine— sat about six feet away. Second, a woman I had seen earlier in the produce section was pushing a cart to the registers. Then I realized what had happened. She had my cart and this lonely one was hers!

I grabbed her cart and took off. For some reason, I thought I had to catch her before she reached the checkout line. As I closed-in on the unwitting cart thief I began to call out, "Ma'am, excuse me, ma'am." By the time I reached her I was out of breath and irritated. As we exchanged carts, I couldn't help but wonder how she had made the mistake. Her cart had about eight or ten items in it—and no purse. But my cart was completely full and contained a suitcase-sized purse in the basket section.

Even though I'm sure she didn't intend to steal my purse, I did learn a lesson. I must be more cautious. Valuable items have to be guarded, not left unprotected.

Most of us naturally protect our physical property and people in our care. We are careful to lock doors, screen babysitters, change the batteries in the smoke detectors, and back up important files on our computers. But how many of us actively work to protect ourselves from temptation?

Right about now, you may be wondering what temptation has to do with standing firm in the midst of life's trials. Every difficult situation is also a time of testing. We are more vulnerable to temptation during the trials of life. In fact, according to the *NIV Application Commentary* on James, the Greek word translated as "trials" in James 1:2 "can mean both incitements to evil thoughts and actions and hardships that prove mettle."

Every hardship we encounter presents us with the same decisions we face in the midst of every temptation. Will we choose our way or God's? Will we trust God or ourselves? Will we rely on the Spirit's power or our own strength? Jesus warned Peter and the other disciples about the danger of temptation and the need to be on guard. But once again, Peter had to learn this lesson through the pain of failure.

UNSHAKEABLE FAITH TRAIT FOUR

Determined to Stay Alert and Guard Against Temptation

LEARNING IT

On the night Jesus was arrested He celebrated the Passover meal with His disciples. After instituting the Lord's Supper in the Upper Room, Jesus led them out to the Mount of Olives. On the way, He tried to prepare them for the trial ahead.

Read Mark 14:27–31. **Jesus shared a lot of important facts in these few verses. Fill in the blanks in the statements below to complete them accurately. Choose from the words/phrases provided.**

three rise away disown dead fall	All the disciples would _____ _____.
	Peter would _____ Jesus _____ times before the night was over.
	Jesus would _____ from the _____ and meet them in Galilee.

✠ Peter reacted strongly to Jesus' statements. Write Peter's bold declarations (vv. 29 and 31) in your own words below.

Do you know someone like Peter? Passionate, outspoken, and so absolutely sure of himself? I've known people like that. And honestly, there have been moments when I *was* people like that! (Another reason I have a soft spot for Peter.)

One word that leaps to mind when I read Peter's declarations is *bravado*. According to Merriam-Webster's online dictionary, *bravado* is "blustering, swaggering conduct; a pretense of bravery."

What do you think caused Peter's bravado?

I feel sure Peter wanted to stand firm with Jesus no matter what happened. He desperately hoped he would be strong enough to cling to Christ, even if it meant arrest or death. Peter was willing to be willing. But Peter still relied on himself and his own strength. He thought he could do it.

Read Mark 14:32–42.

Just moments away from arrest, Jesus confided in His three closest friends that His soul was "overwhelmed with sorrow to the point of death." According to Walter W. Wessel in *The Expositor's Bible Commentary*, this phrase describes an acute emotion that is a painful mixture of bewilderment, fear, uncertainty, and anxiety. In the midst of His severe distress, Jesus needed His friends.

What did Jesus ask Peter, James, and John to do? Circle all that are correct.

Keep watch   Sharpen their swords   Take a nap

Stay   Pray   Resist temptation

Read the definitions of key words from Mark 14:32–42 to help answer the next three questions.

KEY WORDS FROM MARK 14:32-42

Watch — to rouse, to watch, to refrain from sleep; to be mindful of threatening dangers which, with conscious earnestness and an alert mind, keeps one from all drowsiness and all slackening in the energy of faith and conduct

Spirit — the immaterial, invisible part of a man; the element in man by which he perceives, reflects, feels, desires

Flesh — the human body; the infirmity of human nature; the corrupt nature of man subject to the filthy appetites and passions

Note: From *The Complete Word Study New Testament* by Spiros Zodhiates (AMG Publishers, Chattanooga, 1991).

Using what you learned from the definitions, explain what Jesus wanted Peter, James, and John to do when He commanded them to *"keep watch."*

How could *"praying"* and *"watching"* help them to withstand temptation?

❧ What insight does Jesus' statement *"the spirit is willing, but the body is weak"* give us about Peter's bold declaration?

Did you notice what Jesus called Peter in verse 37? In his own strength, Simon could not obey the Master's command to watch and pray. Instead, he succumbed to the weakness of his physical body. The "rock" was nowhere in sight.

Read Mark 14:43–50. **How did Peter and the other disciples once again demonstrate that *"the spirit is willing, but the body is weak"*? (Note: We've read this same story before, but this time we'll make a different application.)**

Using what you've learned, mark the following statements with a T for true and an F for false.

___ Peter and the others planned to desert Jesus all along.
___ Peter believed he could stand firm even in the threat of physical danger.
___ Peter tried to withstand temptation by sheer willpower.

The disciples wanted to stand with Jesus but in the face of physical danger they were tempted to run. And run they did. Like the disciples, we all experience times of physical weakness. Our bodies can only do so much. And, like the disciples, we also experience moral and spiritual weakness. We are constantly tempted to give into sinful desires that arise from our own corrupted human nature. That's why prayer and watchfulness are vital components in our battle against sin.

Read Mark 14:66–72. How did Peter's behavior fulfill Jesus' prophecy in Mark 14:30?

Compare Mark 14:72 with Luke 22:61. What additional information do you find in Luke?

Why do you think Peter *"broke down and wept"*? Check the most accurate statement.

___ He was sorry Jesus had been arrested.
___ He was grieved and repentant over his own behavior.
___ He wished Jesus had not seen him there.

Although Peter fled from danger in the Garden, he loved Jesus too much to stay away. His presence there in the courtyard tells us that much. But the flesh is still weak. Peter's fear for his personal safety once again overrode his love for his Savior.

> Amid all Peter's stumbles and falls this always brought him right again and set him on his feet again—his absolutely enthusiastic love and adoration for his Master.
>
> Alexander Whyte, *Bible Characters*

TEACHING IT

Peter faced an overwhelming trial that tested his faith. He may have fallen to temptation in the Garden and the courtyard but he did learn from his failure. In turn, he wanted others to learn from his experience and not make the same mistakes.

⊰ *Read 1 Peter 5:5b–9.* **In verses 6–9 Peter made four exhortations or "strong, urgent recommendations." Each verse begins with one. List them below.**

1. _____

2. _____

3. _____

4. _____

Did you sense Peter's passion behind these exhortations? I can hear him adding, *Take my word for it; I know. Don't make the same mistakes I did!* Peter's audience was already experiencing trials and persecution. Since suffering of all kinds provides opportunities for Satan to tempt God's children, Peter faithfully shared his hard-earned wisdom to help them stand firm.

I got so excited when I studied this passage. I discovered some things I can hardly wait for you to see! First, let's consider *pride*. Fill in the blank as a reminder: God _____ the proud but gives grace to the _____ .

How did Peter demonstrate pride in Mark 14?

How did we also see Peter humble himself under God's mighty hand?

Peter had a close, personal relationship with our enemy, pride. He proudly declared he would never desert Christ—only to do so later the same night. In his pride, he missed God's grace to stand firm through that trial. But after Peter repented and humbled himself under God's mighty hand, he experienced full restoration with Christ.

⇥ Describe a time in your own life you let pride get the upper hand. In what ways did you feel God's "opposition"?

Peter also saw a need to remind his readers of God cares for them. Whether we are facing an illness, material need, a strained relationship, or Christian persecution, God knows and cares. He invites us to bring our hurts to Him.

⇥ Why did Peter need to remind his readers—and us—that God cares about our struggles?

⌘ What might we be tempted to do if we doubt God's loving concern for us?

Now, here's the little tidbit that really made me smile. In the NIV, the first part of verse 8 reads, *"Be self-controlled and alert."* That word *alert* is the very same Greek word translated as the word *watch* in Mark 14. Jesus' warning to Peter did have an impact!

Describe the enemy we are to "watch out" for and resist.

Peter was a teacher who learned his lessons in the trenches. He knew Satan's tactics first hand. Our enemy the devil will not tiptoe by while we sleep. No, he will devour the unsuspecting and the unprepared. And pride is like the smell of blood to this predator.

LIVING IT

The trials of life can tempt us to be less than completely submitted and obedient to God. Sometimes we don't trust Him enough to continue to follow Him down a hard path. Sometimes we try to fix our problems the world's way or in our own strength instead of depending on God. In essence, we give up on God too quickly and resort to self-preservation. Oh, but no one can care for us better than the Eternal Preserver.

Sadly, sometimes our trials are of our own making. When we disobey God, choose our own way, or fail to guard the weak areas of our lives, the results can be hazardous. And we certainly have enough trouble in this fallen world without causing more for ourselves!

Read 1 Corinthians 10:1–13.

Paul used the Israelites' experience in the wilderness to teach Christians a vital truth: God expects obedience and disobedience brings consequences. The Israelites were God's children. He redeemed them from slavery, guided them with His presence, and provided for their spiritual and physical needs. Sound familiar?

In spite of God's loving care most of that generation never entered the Promised Land. Why?

⊰⊱ Why did Paul give this example? (See vv. 6 and 11.)

Does verse 12 remind you of anyone? *"So, if you think you are stand-ing firm, be careful that you don't fall!"* Peter was certain he would stand firm, but instead he fell. He failed to pray for God's direction and help. He failed to watch out for Satan and his schemes.

Things have not changed since Adam and Eve snacked on the forbidden fruit. Trials and pain still plague people's lives. And that great serpent, the devil, still prowls around trying to entice God's people into disobedience. But, praise God, He has not changed either!

What wonderful promise do you see in verse 13?

You and I do not have to give in to temptation. God always provides a way for us to choose obedience. We don't sin by enduring trials and facing temptation. We do sin when we reject God's way and choose our own.

⤐ Spend a few minutes thinking about your own life. What decisions lay before you today?

Which choice will you make? Circle one:

My way   God's way

God's way will not always be the easiest way or quickest fix, but it will be the best way. He longs to give you the guidance you need in your everyday life—when times are easy and in the midst of trials.

Read "Faith Shaker and then answer the questions that follow.

FAITH SHAKER

Ten years ago, Dana's husband, Mark, quit his full-time job to start a car detail business. But the business didn't do well. Dana soon found herself selling makeup and working catering events, in addition to her full-time secretarial job, to help pay the bills. But even that wasn't enough. They used credit cards to pay bills and buy necessities.

Soon they were deep in debt. They owed more on their house than what it was worth. Mark's truck was repossessed. And the creditors wouldn't stop calling. Dana was so tired of telling them she didn't have the money to pay the bills. The phone calls were a constant reminder of the trouble they were in, so Dana simply stopped answering the phone.

The stress on their marriage was overwhelming. They had to take drastic action. They sold the business, but barely got enough to pay a few bills. They couldn't pay their mortgage and couldn't afford to sell the house for a loss, so they gave it to the bank. They consolidated their credit-card debt and started a payment plan. Then they took a job as house parents at a group home in another state. Still it took them years to recover.

Although much of what they suffered could have happened to anyone trying to start a new business, God showed Dana how her own attitudes and actions were part of the problem. She didn't like to deny herself nice things. And she didn't want to wait for anything. For example, Dana rationalized the additional expense of a new car when a used one would have been more in their budget.

Now, a decade later, Mark and Dana are still learning how to make solid financial decisions. But they know from Scripture and experience how important it is to be on their guard. It's too easy to let materialism and desire for instant gratification override good stewardship.

God shaped and strengthened Dana's faith during these years. She also learned that God is faithful even when she makes mistakes.

Unshakeable Faith

Were Dana and Mark's financial problems entirely their fault? Explain how sin made matters worse?

In what ways has your own sin complicated a difficult situation?

Looking back, what difference would choosing God's way instead have made?

Dana longed to have nice things even if she couldn't afford them. Satan attacked at the point of her weakness and she yielded. She had failed to watch and strengthen the areas where she was vulnerable.

What areas of your life are weak and make you susceptible to temptation?

List some specific ways you can protect or guard these weaknesses? (For example, Dana's weakness was a desire for material things. She was tempted to buy what she didn't need with money she didn't have. Dana could have closed her credit accounts or restricted herself to a set amount of cash for discretionary spending.)

As we close this session, commit these areas to God in prayer. Ask Him to strengthen and protect you. And ask Him to show you clearly His "way out" when you are tempted.

WEEK FIVE
A MIGHTY WIND

*Then Peter said, "Silver or gold I do not have, but what I do have
I give you. In the name of Jesus Christ of Nazareth, walk."*

—Acts 3:6

We have lived in some windy places, but the most unusual wind experiences we've had were in Casper, Wyoming. Casper's location, where prairie and mountains meet, seems to form a kind of wind corridor. Regularly the city issues high wind warnings and recommends that high-profile vehicles stay off the outer loop. As the wind whips around

the side of Casper Mountain it first hits one particular section of the loop near our old house at the northwest edge of the city. We often saw vehicles, like 18-wheelers and RVs, lying on their side on the shoulder of the road.

One spring we lost a ten-foot section of wooden fence when the four-inch posts, embedded in concrete, snapped right off at the ground. I say "lost" because we never even found the fence. Our best guess is that it ended up somewhere in South Dakota.

Then there was the time I was nearly knocked out by our trash can. It was one of those huge, plastic contraptions on wheels that the city gives you to take your trash to the curb. Halfway down the driveway the wind caught the lid and flipped it up and over to whack me in the top of the head. I hit my knees and the trash can hit the ground. Not a pretty sight.

But the oddest wind event of all happened one Christmas season to a man in our church. He went to pick up a few items from the grocery store right around the corner from our house. Spruces, firs, and pines lined the outside wall of the store, waiting to become people's Christmas trees. As he walked from his car to the door, a Douglas fir flew out of nowhere knocking him to the ground. Our poor friend got a broken hip for Christmas.

Although we can't see wind, we can certainly see and feel its effects. Its power is unstoppable. In the third chapter of John, Jesus uses wind as an analogy to teach His nighttime visitor Nicodemus about the Holy Spirit. (See John 3:5–8.) The Holy Spirit has the power and authority to do what He pleases. Although we cannot see Him, we can see and feel His activity.

If you are a Christian—if you've entered into a saving relationship with Jesus Christ—it's because the Holy Spirit gave new life to your sin-dead spirit. You were born again by the power of His presence. That same power is now living and active in your life! The Holy Spirit is our gift from the Father. He equips and enables us to live the life God has purposed for us. And that includes standing firm through the storms of life.

In this session we are going to begin to see a marked difference in our friend Peter. Remember, we learned that Peter's spirit was willing to stand with Jesus, but his flesh was weak. In fact, his flesh tucked tail and ran when things got tough. Peter didn't have enough power to stand firm on his own. Now let's see what God could do with Peter after he encounters the Holy Spirit!

UNSHAKEABLE FAITH TRAIT FIVE
Lives by the Power of the Indwelling Holy Spirit

LEARNING IT

When Jesus died, sadness and fear overwhelmed the disciples. Even though Jesus told them many times He would rise from the dead, they didn't understand. (See Luke 18:31–34.) Instead of camping out near the garden tomb anticipating God's miracle, they were grieving behind closed doors.

Read Luke 24:36–43.

How do their reactions demonstrate they were not expecting a visit from Jesus?

How did Jesus prove to Peter and the other disciples that He physically arose from the dead?

Read Luke 24:44–49, compare it to Luke 18:31–34, and then fill in the table below.

	Luke 18:31–34	Luke 24:44–49
Was this before or after Jesus' death?		
What was prophesied about Jesus?		
Where was it written?		
Did the disciples understand what Jesus meant?		
What did Jesus expect them to do with the news?		
When were they to act?		

Jesus' suffering, death, and resurrection may have come as a surprise to the disciples, but not to God. In fact, before the creation of the world, He ordained Christ's sacrifice to provide salvation for all mankind (1 Peter 1:20). Jesus gave Peter and the other disciples the glorious privilege of telling the news. But the task would not be easy. They would need much more than their own strength to carry it out. They would need the very power of God. Read Jesus' last words to the disciples just before He returned to heaven as recorded in Acts 1:8.

↬ How would they receive the power Jesus had promised them?

What would this power enable them to do?

The disciples followed Jesus' instructions and returned to Jerusalem from the Mount of Olives to wait for God's promise. They didn't have to wait long. The Day of Pentecost was only about ten days after Jesus' ascension. Pentecost, which was 50 days after Passover, was one of three Jewish festivals that involved a pilgrimage to Jerusalem. Jews from all over the Roman Empire would have been gathered in the city of David. God provided a huge audience to witness the coming of the Holy Spirit. Doesn't He have great timing?

↬ *Read Acts 2:1–8.* How is the Holy Spirit's arrival described in verses 2–3?

It's not a coincidence that the Holy Spirit is compared to the wind once again. In fact, the Greek word translated as "spirit" can also

Unshakeable Faith

be translated as "wind." *The Complete Word Study New Testament* defines *pneuma* this way: "to breathe, blow; primarily denotes the wind. Breath; the spirit which, like the wind, is invisible, immaterial, and powerful." The use of the adjective "violent" or "mighty" in Acts 2:8 adds the characteristics of strength and power.

Which of the believers gathered there were filled with the Holy Spirit? Circle one answer.

Only Peter   Only the apostles   All the believers

<del>⇥</del> What is significant about the fact that tongues of fire separated and settled on each believer individually?

How did the Holy Spirit demonstrate His presence and power in the believers on the Day of Pentecost?

If you belong to Christ, you have the indwelling presence of the Holy Spirit. (See Romans 8:9–11.) As the Spirit enabled those first Christians on Pentecost to follow Jesus in obedience, He will enable you. Now let's look in on the Spirit-filled Peter.

<del>⇥</del> *Read Acts 2:14, 36–41.* **What difference do you see in Peter compared to the night Jesus was arrested? Particularly note the descriptive verbs in verse 40.**

In week four, we experienced Peter's desertion and denial of Christ. Willing in spirit, but weak in flesh he could not stand firm in his own strength. Fifty days later Peter stood in front of a crowd of thousands. Empowered and emboldened by the Holy Spirit, he pointed out their sin and called them to repentance. Simon the fisherman was now Peter the Rock.

> After Pentecost we see a different Peter — Peter, filled with the Holy Spirit and driven by the knowledge that Christ had risen from the dead, had acquired an unshakeable, rock-solid courage.
>
> John MacArthur
> *Twelve Ordinary Men*

TEACHING IT

Peter was empowered by the Holy Spirit to proclaim the gospel message with courage and boldness. The result? Three thousand people were saved in one day. And effective preaching was only the beginning.

Read Acts 3:1–10.

The early Jerusalem Christians continued to worship God at the temple. One day on their way to afternoon prayer, Peter and John encountered a lame beggar. Since almsgiving was considered a virtuous act, beggars regularly positioned themselves to intercept worshippers on their way to the temple.

⤷ Why do you think the Scriptures make a point of telling us the man had been lame from birth?

What did the man want that Peter lacked?

What did the man need that Peter had?

When Peter demanded the man's attention, he looked up with expectation. Maybe these two Galileans would give him enough money to buy bread for his supper. But this lame beggar expected too little. He hoped for only a full belly, not knowing that Peter and John had access to something far more valuable—the power to heal.

Read Acts 3:11–16.

By whose power was the lame man healed? Check the correct answer.
___ Peter and John
___ Abraham, Isaac, and Jacob
___ Jesus

Peter made it clear to all that the man was healed in the name of *Jesus*. In ancient Jewish thought a person's name expressed his very nature. Therefore, to heal in the name of Jesus means he called upon the power and authority of Jesus Himself. Peter refused to take the glory for himself.

The miracle of physical healing was only one aspect of the Spirit's work. Peter continued to pass along everything he learned about the power of the Holy Spirit in a believer's life.

➳ In 2 Peter 1:3, Peter wrote that God's *"divine power has given us everything we need for a godly life."* Read the surrounding passage, 2 Peter 1:3–11, and then read Romans 8:9–11 to identify the believer's source of *"divine power."* From where does it come?

⇥ Now, look back at 2 Peter 1:4. According to this verse, what do we escape when we "participate in the divine nature"?

God saved us with purposeful intent. He intends for us to become like Jesus, to be *"conformed to the likeness of his Son"* (Romans 8:29). God demands our cooperation, but the Holy Spirit supplies the power to accomplish this sanctifying work. And this power is the very same power that raised Jesus from the dead! (See Romans 8:11.)

Peter recognized that God, through the indwelling presence of the Holy Spirit, gives believers everything we need to live the life He calls us to live. Whatever our circumstances, physical weaknesses, limited material resources, or emotional needs, God will supply. I don't know about you, but I sometimes find it easier to be "godly" when life is stress-free. But when problems and heartaches begin to mount, my weak flesh rears its ugly head. (Remember our discussion last week that every hardship of life is also a time of testing and temptation.)

Even as I write this lesson, I'm struggling with a situation that requires patience and selfless love. Yet every day I realize how impatient, selfish, and unloving I am. My spirit wants to keep giving, but like Peter, my flesh is weak.

Oh, but wait! God's Word declares that I have everything I need to escape my selfish, evil desires and act like Jesus. As I step out in obedience, the Holy Spirit will empower me to act godly in this difficult situation.

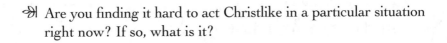 Are you finding it hard to act Christlike in a particular situation right now? If so, what is it?

What do you feel you are lacking in order to respond like Christ would?

Reread 2 Peter 1:3–4. **What does God's Word promise you? Put it in your own handwriting!**

The Holy Spirit Is God in Us

Peter calls the Holy Spirit "God"	Acts 5:3–4
The Holy Spirit was active in creation	Genesis 1:2
The Holy Spirit is omnipresent — everywhere simultaneously	Psalm 139:7–8
The Holy Spirit is omniscient — all-knowing	1 Corinthians 2:10–12
The Holy Spirit gives eternal life	John 3:5–7
The Holy Spirit is eternal	Hebrews 9:14
The Holy Spirit gives us access to the Father	Ephesians 2:18
God's Spirit, the Holy Spirit, lives in believers	1 Corinthians 3:16

Living It

> The Holy Spirit resides within you, the believer, to give you the staying power you need to grow steadily and remain steadfast in your faith regardless of circumstances around you or feelings that ebb and flow like the tide.
>
> Charles Stanley
> *Living in the Power of the Holy Spirit*

Even though God has supplied me with everything I need to act like Christ and stand firm in every situation, I often still fall. And I'm pretty sure I know why. If you have the same trouble, maybe the Scripture that spoke to me will be helpful to you as well.

Earlier we read Romans 8:9–11. Now let's read the larger section, verses 5–12. Check each of the following statements that reflect truths found in this passage.

___ When I sin, it is because my own desires are more important to me than God's will.

___ When I choose my own way over God's way, it often results in more problems and grief.

___ When God's will is my priority, I will follow the Spirit's guidance.

___ When I allow God's Spirit to control my life, He will fill me with His peace.

___ As a Christian—born again by the Spirit of God—I am obligated to live by the Spirit.

Although biblical scholars debate whether Paul was referring to Christians or non-Christians in verses 5–8, I believe the principles still apply to those of us who have been saved but sometimes struggle with our old sin natures. When I fail to act godly—even though I have everything I need for godliness through the indwelling of the Holy Spirit—it's because I want what I want, the way I want it. I choose to feed my selfish desires. But when I choose obedience and submit myself to the Holy Spirit's control, I also open myself to His power and blessing.

Look back at the statements in the question above. Underline the ones that most accurately reflect your life right now. In the midst of a trial, do you more often resemble "the sinful nature" or the Spirit?

⫸ The Bible is full of passages about the role of the Holy Spirit in a believer's life. But for our purposes today, let's focus on a few Scriptures that show how the Holy Spirit works in the midst of our trials. Read the following passages and fill in the table. (I've filled in the first one to get you started.)

SCRIPTURE	LIFE SITUATION	HOLY SPIRIT'S WORK/BENEFITS
Luke 12:11–12	Testifying about Christ	I don't have to worry about what to say. He will give me the words.
John 14:25–27		
Acts 1:8		
Romans 8:26–27		
2 Corinthians 4:7–9		
2 Timothy 1:7–8		

The Holy Spirit still works today like He worked in the lives of those first-century Christians. He is able and ready to provide us with everything we need for every situation we face today.

Read "Faith Shaker" for a real-life example of how He still works today.

FAITH SHAKER

How does a mom keep going when she knows she could lose her son any moment? Wende's answer comes without hesitation. "I couldn't have done this for five minutes without God."

Ethan was diagnosed with an extremely rare condition when he was just ten years old. Arteriovenous malformation (AVM), an abnormal formation of blood vessels in the brain, can cause seizures, hemorrhages, and strokes. Larger AVMs, like Ethan's, result in progressive neurological deterioration. And a ruptured aneurysm is a daily possibility.

Wende smiles when she describes Ethan's early childhood years. In the gifted program at school, he could beat his dad at chess, and loved to write and garden. Ethan was a beautiful and happy child with a contagious grin.

There was no hint of a problem until ten-year-old Ethan's hands started shaking. It took eight months and several doctors before they received the AVM diagnosis. Shortly after that he suffered a stroke.

The stroke left Ethan with some physical challenges, but it did not weaken his spirit or his faith in God. He never asked "Why me?" Instead Ethan firmly believed that God wanted to use his illness for a specific purpose.

Wende agrees completely. "I've seen God use Ethan to change people's lives. They've caught his joy. He loved people just the way they are. The way he lived taught people not to get caught up in things that don't really matter."

But how did Ethan's mom cope? Wende remembers a specific moment only days after the diagnosis. "I was washed by an overwhelming sense of God's peace and I felt God whisper, 'I've got this.' And I believed Him."

The Holy Spirit continued to pour peace into Wende's life. "Those moments were a rest from all the things I had to deal with, so I could keep going."

Wende experienced the Holy Spirit working in other ways as well. Joy when she was grieving. Strength when she felt weak. The constant awareness of God's presence and love. And the physical support of God's people.

After nine years of battling AVM, Ethan went home to heaven. Today—the day after Ethan's memorial service—Wende is choosing to cling to the peace God continues to provide.

In the midst of her heartbreaking trial, do you think Wende also faced any temptations? If so, what?

How did the Holy Spirit help Wende endure the illness and loss of her son?

Can you recall a time when the Spirit worked in your life in a similar way? If so, describe it below.

Peter learned by experience that God provides through His Spirit everything a believer needs for life and godliness. Are you experiencing that now? Are there situations in your life that still need to be empowered and overpowered by the power of God's Spirit?

Unshakeable Faith

Before you close your book today, write a prayer below. List your current life situations in which you need a fresh encounter with the Spirit of God. Ask God for His power, strength, peace, and guidance now.

Week Six

Spring Cleaning

But just as he who called you is holy, so be holy in all you do.
—1 Peter 1:15

y daughter Kelley and I have a sweet, close relationship. But there have been a few times over her 23 years of life when things were strained between us. Silence, distance, and even irritation marked these periods. Thankfully, these times were very few and relatively short!

In almost every instance the trouble in our relationship started because Kelley knew I wouldn't approve of something she was doing. She didn't want me "meddling" in her business so she hid her behavior by "hiding" from me.

I've experienced the same in my relationship with God. There have been seasons when I avoided Him because I didn't want to hear what He had to say to me. I was determined to go my own way so I didn't pray, I didn't read His Word. I wanted to do life my way, not God's way, so I pulled away from Him. I was still His child, but I experienced no sweet fellowship, no sense of His presence. It's impossible to be intimate with God and be rebellious at the same time.

Why do we rob ourselves of everything God wants to give us? He longs to fill our lives with the peace, comfort, and joy of His presence but too many times we've distanced ourselves from Him. When we allow our lives to become cluttered and messy with the stuff of this world, we ruin the intimate fellowship with our heavenly Father.

Peter wrote clearly and passionately about a Christian's need for holiness. He learned this truth firsthand from Jesus. And he faithfully taught it to the church. Let's dig in. This one's too important to miss!

LEARNING IT

In Peter's day, no one was considered more holy and righteous than the Pharisees. The people looked to them as the example to follow. If you wanted to be close to God and experience His blessings, then you wanted to be like the Pharisees. But Jesus knew the truth. Many of the Pharisees only looked good on the surface. And Peter was there when Jesus told them to clean up their act.

Read Matthew 23:23–28. **Describe how the typical Pharisee looked to the outward observer.**

⇒ Now describe what Jesus saw when He looked past the outward facade to the inner person. (Read the sidebar "Clean Inside and Out" to help with your answer.)

What did Jesus tell the Pharisees to do in verse 26?

Based on Jesus' description of the Pharisees and the definition of clean what does this look like in a spiritual sense?

Clean Inside and Out

God wants us, His children, to be "clean" inside and out. So what does that look like? Consider the definitions below of the Greek words translated as "clean" in this section's Scripture passages. Looking at the original language can help us get a better understanding of God's standard of "clean."

Clean/cleanse (*katharizo*), verb, found in Matthew 23:25 and 23:26

To make clean, cleanse from physical stains and dirt
To make clean, cleanse in a moral sense
- To free from defilement of sin and from faults
- To purify from wickedness
- To free from guilt of sin, to purify
- To consecrate by cleansing or purifying

Clean/pure (*katharos*), adjective, found in Matthew 23:26 and Matthew 5:8

Clean, pure physically
Clean, pure ethically
- Free from corrupt desire, from sin and guilt
- Free from every admixture of what is false, sincere genuine
- Blameless, innocent

Sadly, many of the Pharisees had lost proper focus. Instead of living to please their heavenly Father, they sought to look good in the eyes of men. Pride blinded them and they stumbled into a life of hypocrisy. They had become extremely good at religion, but it cost them an intimate relationship with God (Matthew 23:37).

Jesus made it very clear that the cleanliness of our inner lives is much more important than the spit-shine of our outward appearance. In fact, we don't really have to worry about the outside. If we concentrate on some serious inside housekeeping, the outside will take care of itself.

Jesus emphasized the importance of a "clean" life from the very beginning of His ministry. In fact, not long after He first called Peter, Jesus revealed a glorious benefit for those who are "clean."

SEE THE DIFFERENCE

Does the cleanliness of our lives really matter? Yes! For many reasons! But there is one by-product of a holy life that is especially precious. Check out the definitions below to help unearth this treasure.

See *horao*, verb, found in Matthew 5:8 and Hebrews 12:14

- To see with the eyes
- To see with the mind, to perceive, know
- To see, become acquainted with by experience, to experience

Holiness (*hagiasmos*), noun, found in Hebrews 12:14

- Consecration, purification
- The effect of consecration, the sanctification (set apart to God) of heart and life

Read Matthew 5:8. (Note: The word *pure* in Matthew 5:8 is translated from the same Greek adjective translated as "clean" in Matthew 23:26.)

❂ After reading "See the Difference," review the definition for *pure* given above in "Clean Inside and Out." Use this information to write an expanded version of Matthew 5:8.

Now read Hebrews 12:14b and compare it to Matthew 5:8. **What does the Hebrews passage add to our understanding of what it means to be** *"pure in heart"*? **(See the definition for** *holiness* **to help with your answer.)**

⊰ In what ways can a deeper experience with God and a more intimate understanding of Him bless our life and help us in times of trials?

I want to experience as much of God as He will give me! How about you? We've seen from Scripture that those who seek to live a clean, pure, holy life will see God. Are you ready to join me in a little spring cleaning? Before we shine the light on our own lives in "Living It," let's see what Peter learned about holiness from Jesus that he faithfully passed on.

TEACHING IT

I saw something completely out of place one day at the nail salon. Once my nails were safely stuck under the drying light, I shifted into people-watching mode. A middle-aged couple sat at a nearby table. It didn't take me long to access the situation. This well-groomed woman was not happy with the condition of her husband's eyebrows so she had brought him in for a waxing. There is no way I can adequately describe this sight to you. Dressed in jeans, a flannel shirt, and work boots, the poor man looked defeated as he submitted his unruly brows to the salon tech's efforts. Thankfully, my nails dried and I was able to make my exit before things got really sticky.

In our culture, a holy life often stands out like a trucker in a nail salon. Christians who obediently strive to conform to the image of Christ are unique novelties in the midst of the "normal" majority. In the short-term, it's easier for us simply to blend in with the crowd. But Peter knew eternity far outweighs the here and now. He wrote to help us grasp both the reason and the need for holiness.

Read 1 Peter 1:13–16. Peter's call to holy living begins with a "therefore" in verse 13. Look back at 1 Peter 1:3–4, which we studied in week one, to see the wonderful truth that deserves the response of a holy life. Write it below.

∜ Using the information in 1 Peter 1:13–14, draw lines between the two columns below to connect the holy characteristic Peter says God expects in His children to the contrasting worldly characteristic that is so prevalent today.

HOLY CHARACTERISTIC	WORLDLY CHARACTERISTIC
Prepares to actively follow Christ	Seeks to be fulfilled by the world
Self-control	Conforms to the world's desires
Eternal mind-set/hope is in eternity	Unprepared to stand spiritually firm
Obedience to God	Self-indulgent
Nonconformity to the world	Ignores God's commands and guidance

Now reread 1 Peter 1:15–16. **Why does God say we should be holy?**

Children of God should be like their Father. We are to conform to the image of God as seen in Jesus Christ, not to the world and its ways. God calls us to be countercultural when it comes to the ethics, morality, and temporal pursuits of our society. But it won't be easy.

⇥ *Read 1 Peter 1:17–23.* **List additional reasons to live a holy life Peter gave here.**

LIVING IT

It's time for us to get practical. Let's pull out our brooms, mops, and dust rags and get busy on those overlooked corners of our lives. The task may be uncomfortable but God will be pleased with the result!

The Apostle Paul, who agreed wholeheartedly with Peter about holy living, gave some direction in his writings that will help us with our task. There are two particular passages that list many holy and worldly characteristics. May God lovingly use them to shine a light on our own lives.

week 6

❧ *Read Ephesians 4:17–32; Ephesians 5:1–21 and Colossians 3:1–17.* As you read each passage list every character trait you can find in the appropriate column in the table below.

Holy Behavior/ Characteristics	Worldly Behavior/ Characteristics

I want you to know I'm doing this right along with you. God still has a lot of work to do in my life. Before we move ahead, will you pray this prayer with me?

Unshakeable Faith

earch me, God, and know my heart;
test me and know my anxious thoughts.
See if there is any offensive way in me,
and lead me in the way everlasting.
Psalm 139:23–24

Review the table of characteristics.

- Circle any characteristic on the left side that is lacking in your life right now.

- Underline any characteristic on the right side that is present in your life in any amount.

- Spend a few moments in confession and petition. Ask God to forgive any worldliness and to help you pursue holiness through the power of His Spirit.

How do you feel? I'm sort of exhausted. This kind of business with God is never easy, but it's eternally beneficial. Let's look at one of David's Psalms that reminds us of the great blessings of holiness.

Read Psalm 15:1–5. **According to verse 2, who may "dwell in God's sanctuary"?**

God's sanctuary and His holy hill are both symbolic of His presence. To "dwell in His sanctuary" then means we have the unequaled blessing of living in His presence. According to Willem A. VanGemeren in the *Expositor's Bible Commentary*, the "blameless walk is the manner of life characterized by integrity. The word *tamim* (blameless) signifies a moral way of life. It is not synonymous with 'perfect' but with an attitude of the heart desirous of pleasing God." To walk blamelessly is live a holy life!

⊰ Now look at the very last sentence of Psalm 15. What is the outcome for someone whose walk is blameless and who dwells in God's sanctuary?

I love God's Word and His promises! We will continue to face trials, temptations, and difficulties as long as we live in this earthly body. But if we pursue holiness, we will not fall when adversity strikes. We will be unshakeable!

> To pursue holiness is to move toward joy—joy infinitely greater than any earthly delights can offer. To resist holiness or to be half-hearted about its pursuit is to forfeit true joy and to settle for something less than that God-intoxication for which we were created.
>
> Nancy Leigh DeMoss
> *Holiness: The Heart God Purifies*

Read "Faith Shaker" and then answer the questions that follow.

FAITH SHAKER

Julie began to drift away from God when she went away to college. Her family and church friends had encouraged her in her faith and held her accountable. Now that they were several hours away, it didn't take long for Julie to feel that God was distant and uninvolved in her life.

Halfway through the fall semester she began dating Luke. Soon, Julie began to expect things from him for which she should have been relying on God. As Julie grew increasingly dependent on Luke, she allowed their relationship to become sexual.

Julie rationalized her behavior. "I knew that sex outside of marriage is sinful. I told myself it was OK because I was 'in love.' Plus I thought it couldn't be that bad; everyone else was doing it."

Ironically, Luke didn't comfort Julie or make her feel secure. "We both felt guilty. We didn't trust each other. Our relationship was very dramatic and volatile."

Julie's relationship with God went from strained to practically nonexistent. "I never prayed, I never read my Bible. I felt a nagging all the time that I should, but when I ignored the gentle prodding, that got quieter too."

When Luke broke off the relationship, Julie was devastated. But looking back, Julie believes God had finally intervened. God allowed her life to be shaken so Julie would realize all she honestly needed was Him.

After the breakup, sorrow overwhelmed Julie because her life had become something she didn't recognize. "I missed God. I couldn't remember the last time I prayed. That's when I finally cried about that instead of Luke."

Broken, Julie turned to a home group from a local church she had been attending sporadically. Although she had only been shallow and fake with the young women, she now opened up and told them honestly about her life. They graciously encouraged her and became a source of accountability as Julie found her way back into a right relationship with God. Now Julie finds comfort, strength, and security in God alone.

How did Julie's lack of intimacy with God contribute to her falling into a sinful relationship with Luke?

How did Julie's sin cause her to drift even further away from God?

Why do you think Julie was so devastated by the breakup with Luke?

Think about a time in your life when your own sin strained your relationship with God. What brought you to repentance? How did God restore your relationship?

List some reasons why a commitment to holiness can foster a deeper intimacy with God?

I don't want to be far from God when tough times hit. I want to be close enough to God to feel His breath on my cheek and His strong arms around me. What about you? If there is something in your life that's gotten between you and your Savior, don't close this book today without going to Him in repentance. He's right there waiting.

WEEK SEVEN
LET'ER RIP

*But rejoice inasmuch as you participate in the sufferings of Christ,
so that you may be overjoyed when his glory is revealed.*
— 1 Peter 4:13

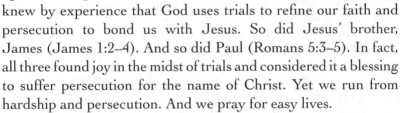

"No pain, no gain." I heard that phrase often during my college years. My friends and I spent many hours working out with Jane Fonda, the exercise guru of the 1980s, and feeling "the burn." Of course Fonda did not discover the reality that strength grows from enduring difficulty. She merely used the truth to coin a phrase that helped sell millions of videos.

We see this truth again and again in Scripture. Our friend Peter knew by experience that God uses trials to refine our faith and persecution to bond us with Jesus. So did Jesus' brother, James (James 1:2–4). And so did Paul (Romans 5:3–5). In fact, all three found joy in the midst of trials and considered it a blessing to suffer persecution for the name of Christ. Yet we run from hardship and persecution. And we pray for easy lives.

Christians around the world are imprisoned, beaten, and even killed because they claim the name of Christ. We hear stories regularly from places like China, North Korea, Pakistan, and India. But persecution such as that hasn't yet happened in the US. At least not like it happens in other parts of the world. Should we be glad?

Recently I read an archived *Baptist Press* article by James T. Draper. In the article, Draper recounts a Christian reporter's conversation with a prominent leader of the Chinese house church movement. When the reporter asked him how US Christians could pray for Chinese Christians he responded passionately. "Stop praying for persecution in China to end, for it is through persecution that the church has grown. We, in fact, are praying that the American church might taste the same persecution so revival would come to the American church like we have seen in China."

God has used many of life's trials and difficulties to shape and refine my faith. But, I must admit, other than some teasing and mild ridicule I've never been persecuted solely because I stood up for the name of Christ. However, I've often wondered how I would respond. I pray that my words and actions would honor Christ and that I would not look for an easy way out.

It doesn't take a prophet to know that views are changing about Christians in the US. All you have to do is turn on the television or go online. We have lost favor with popular culture, and the only thing that is not tolerated in our tolerant society is Christianity. Increasing persecution in various forms could soon find us, right here at home. How will you respond when it comes?

UNSHAKEAßLE FAITH TRAIT SEVEN

Prepared to Endure Persecution for the Sake of Christ

LEARNING IT

Jesus did not shy away from the subject of persecution. He clearly taught Peter and the other apostles that they would suffer because they followed Him. Although, He warned them to be on guard, He also promised they wouldn't have to worry about what to say. The Holy Spirit would give them the right words at the right time. (See Matthew 10:17–20 and Mark 13:9–11.)

⤷ *Read John 15:18–21.* **List all the reasons Jesus gives in this passage that explains why the world will persecute His followers.**

⊰⊱ *Read John 7:7.* **What additional information do you learn in this verse about the reason for Christian persecution?**

Jesus warned His disciples as a group about persecution through-out His ministry and even on the night He was betrayed. Yet, after the Resurrection, Jesus specifically singled out Peter regarding some future suffering.

One morning, after a night of fishing, Jesus appeared to Peter and some of the other disciples on the shore of the Sea of Galilee. Jesus had cooked breakfast and had it waiting for them. After they ate, Jesus turned His attention to Peter. After denying Christ on the night of His trial, Peter needed reassurance that Jesus could still use him. Jesus not only reconfirmed Peter's call to serve His church, He also warned him about some personal suffering ahead.

As mentioned earlier in this study, based on church tradition and writings of some early church fathers, it is generally accepted that Peter died a martyr's death under Nero's persecutions in Rome. These sources tell that after first witnessing his wife's martyrdom, Peter was crucified head downward because he felt unworthy to die in the same manner Christ died.

Read John 21:18–19. **How do Jesus' words reflect what we believe happened to Peter at the end of his life?**

Not long after this encounter on the beach Jesus returned to heaven and the Holy Spirit arrived. From that time on Peter and the other disciples boldly proclaimed the good news of Jesus. And though their testimony regularly earned them beatings and imprisonment, they joyfully endured.

> After Christ's death, the disciples had to hold fast to what they believed concerning God's Son. In the end, the adversity they faced led to an increased joy that came through the reality of living in harmony with the Holy Spirit.
>
> Charles Stanley
> *Into His Presence*

Read Acts 5:17–42.

There are several important things in this passage we don't want to miss. But before we forge ahead, let's take one step back to set the stage. Acts 5:17 tells us the Jewish leaders were jealous of Peter and the other apostles. Let's see some reasons why.

Read Acts 5:12–16. **Check all the statements below that, based on this passage, could have caused the Jewish leaders to be jealous of the apostles.**

___The apostles performed miracles, healed the sick, and cast out demons.

___The apostles were highly regarded by all the people.

___The church continued to grow.

___The apostles had a lot of money.

Unshakeable Faith

⊰ฬ Look again at Acts 5:17–42. What did Peter and the other apostles suffer at the hands of the Jewish leaders?

How did God act on their behalf?

What command did God give the apostles? What command did the Jewish leaders give them?

How did Peter and the apostles respond to God? To the Jewish leaders?

⊰ฬ *Reread verse 41.* **Explain why Peter and the others rejoiced when they were persecuted.**

It certainly seems odd that suffering for Christ could bring joy. Yet spiritual truth often contradicts the wisdom and logic of this world. Peter experienced both the pain of persecution and the joy that results from suffering for the name of Christ. This testing also refined and strengthened Peter's faith. Good-bye shifting sand, hello solid rock!

TEACHING IT

Before we look specifically at Peter's teaching on persecution, let's take a moment to see what he taught about how God uses difficulties in the lives of His children. As we move ahead, you may find yourself wondering if we're talking about temptation or life's trials. The answer is yes.

Remember, we discovered the close connection between life's trials and temptations in week four. We learned that every temptation tests our faith and each trial entices us to choose our way over God's. The Greek word translated as "trials" in 1 Peter 1:6 (and in James 1:2) can refer to both hardships and temptation to sin.

Read 1 Peter 1:3–9.

We studied the first part of this passage in week one. Peter begins by eloquently expressing the greatness of our glorious salvation. We have been given new birth and the hope of an eternal inheritance. God shields and protects us through this life while He moves us forward toward the ultimate fulfillment of that spiritual goal to be revealed when Jesus returns.

But while we wait for God's promises, we will have to *"suffer grief in all kinds of trials."* Why? Why do we have to experience difficulties and endure the trials of life? Every person who has ever lived has probably asked that very question. Although I believe we will never fully understand on this side of eternity, God does give us some answers in His Word. So let's learn what we can and trust Him for the rest.

✠ Use 1 Peter 1:3–9 to explain and elaborate on the following statements.

We can have joy in the midst of trials.

Trials are only temporary.

God uses our trials for His purposes.

Read the passages from James and Romans below and add the information you find there about how God works through trials to shape our faith.

James 1:2–4:

Romans 5:3–5:

In recent years, as I've studied about God's discipline and how He works through trials, suffering, and persecution in the lives of His children, I've come to what I believe is a very biblical conclusion: God allows these things in our lives and uses them to refine us spiritually because He cares more about our spiritual condition than He does our physical condition. At first I found this hard to accept. Since I struggle sometimes to keep an eternal perspective, I often find myself worrying much more about the here and now. If you have the same trouble, check out "God's Priority" to see what Jesus had to say about it.

GOD'S PRIORITY

Jesus made it very clear that God cares about every aspect of our physical lives. He knows we need food and clothes. He promises to provide for our physical needs.

"So don't worry about [having enough food or drink or clothing]. . . . your heavenly Father already knows all your needs. Seek the Kingdom of God above all else, and live righteously, and he will give you everything you need" (Matthew 6:31–33 NLT).

But as much as He cares about our physical well-being, He cares even more about our spiritual well-being.

Our spiritual condition is God's priority. Jesus said it should also be *our* priority.

Scripture clearly shows us that everyone — the believer and unbeliever alike — will experience temptation, trials, and difficulties as the due course of a fallen world. But God doesn't waste these things in a Christian's life. He uses them to refine our faith, shape our character, and transform us to the image of Christ.

Trials may be common to all humans, but Christian persecution is unique. Only those who claim Christ as Lord and follow Him will experience it. This persecution is a direct result of obedience to God. For the reasons we studied earlier, the unbelieving world sometimes reacts to the presence of Christ in His people with opposition and hostility.

⊰ *Read 1 Peter 3:13–17.* **List all the instructions Peter gives about how a Christian should prepare for and respond to persecution.**

- •

- •

- •

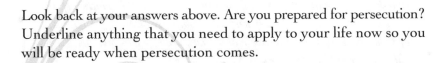

Look back at your answers above. Are you prepared for persecution? Underline anything that you need to apply to your life now so you will be ready when persecution comes.

Peter also mentions two results of persecution — one for the persecuted and one for the persecutor. Fill in the blanks in the following statements to complete the results.

If you should suffer for doing what is right, you are _____ _____ (v. 14).

Those who malign your good behavior in Christ may be _____ _____ (v. 16).

Read Matthew 5:10–12. **How does Peter's teaching reflect Jesus' teaching?**

Peter endured decades of malicious slander, beatings, and imprisonment because in his heart he had "set apart Christ as Lord." Never again would he deny His name. Never again would he run away. The rock-solid foundation of Peter's faith provided an unshakeable place for him to stand firm for the cause of Christ.

Living It

Think about one of your close friends. How did your relationship develop beyond a simply casual friendship? Besides spending a lot of time with each other, it's likely that the two of you have also shared some difficult experiences. Perhaps you helped her through an illness or she grieved with you over a loss.

Intimacy is often forged in common pain. That's why the Apostle Paul passionately proclaimed, *"I want to know Christ . . . the power of his resurrection and participation in his sufferings, becoming like him in his death"* (Philippians 3:10). Paul longed to know Jesus in a way that comes only through sharing with Christ the experience of His persecution. Additionally, Paul understood that God has great purpose in allowing persecution in the lives of His children.

Read 2 Corinthians 4:7–12. **Why did Paul refer to himself as a** *"jar of clay"* **in verse 7?**

How does God reveal His power through us to the world in the midst of suffering and persecution?

How do you feel about the possibility of persecution in your own life? Would you run from it or face it boldly? Peter gives us clear advice about suffering for the name of Christ.

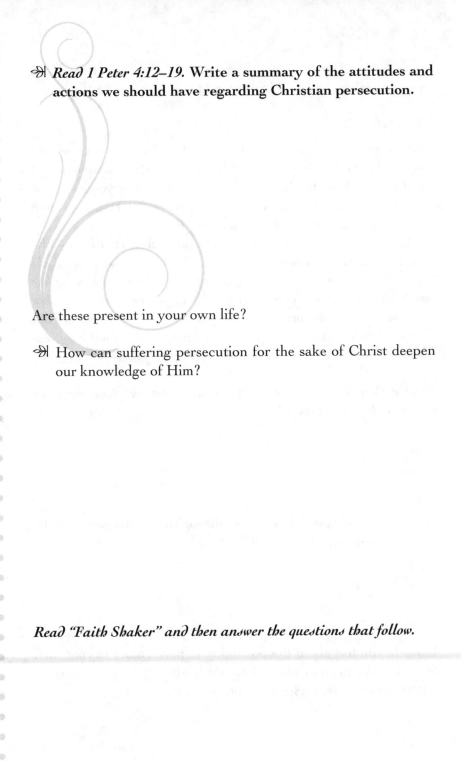

⇥ *Read 1 Peter 4:12–19.* Write a summary of the attitudes and actions we should have regarding Christian persecution.

Are these present in your own life?

⇥ How can suffering persecution for the sake of Christ deepen our knowledge of Him?

Read "Faith Shaker" and then answer the questions that follow.

FAITH SHAKER

Lauren never expected to experience Christian persecution in her college history class. But from the very first day, the professor expressed his contempt for anything and everything Christian. He told the class he had once been a seminary student but dropped out when he realized that "religion is only lies, just a game for fools." Almost every class period the professor threw in some negative remark about God, Christians, or the Bible.

His comments remained directed to no one in particular until about halfway through the semester during a lesson on segregation, racism, and the Ku Klux Klan (KKK). When the professor flashed up a photo of three robed KKK members, he asked any Christians in the class to stand up. Lauren looked around at the class of more than 60 students. Only she and one young man were on their feet.

The professor spent the next 20 minutes blaming Lauren's faith and her God for the injustices committed by violent, hateful men. The young man remained silent when the professor asked for a response, but Lauren felt she had to speak. She told the professor and the class that her God loves all people and calls her to love them as well.

As the semester continued, God helped Lauren every time the professor asked her to defend her faith. "I began to enjoy the weekly encounters with my professor. He eventually became less challenging and seemed to be curious because I never backed down."

Although Lauren realizes she needs to better equip herself for similar persecution she may face in the future, she knows her faith grew through the experience. "God provided me with the strength and the words to handle the situation with love and not anger. Intellectually, I knew He promised to be with us, but I had never experienced His presence like that before. Now I want to know Him even more."

In what specific ways did God help Lauren respond to her professor's persecution?

How was Lauren's faith strengthened through the experience?

Do you think this persecution will change how Lauren lives out her faith in the future? If so, in what ways?

The United States has entered a post-Christian era. My parents — and even I — grew up in a time when faith and church attendance were not only socially acceptable; they were commended. But times are drastically different today. For the most part, Christians are considered to be intolerant and ignorant by our main stream culture.

List several ways that believers in the United States today are persecuted for their faith.

Do you think it is possible for a Christian in America to be completely obedient to Christ and not suffer any form of persecution?

___ Yes.

___ No.

___ I'm not sure.

Do you desire to know Christ more fully? Are you willing to suffer for His name? As we close this session, spend some time in prayer. Ask God to prepare your heart and mind for possible persecution and to give you the strength and courage to be unshakeable in the midst of it.

Week Eight

Share the Love

Now that you have purified yourselves by obeying the truth so that you have sincere love for your brothers, love one another deeply, from the heart.

—1 Peter 1:22

The church we were members of in Casper, Wyoming, had a certain reputation in the community. It was a well-attested fact that the members of College Heights Baptist Church greatly loved and cared for each other. For  example, the staff of the local hospital knew that if one person from College Heights was admitted or came into the emergency room that the waiting room would soon be full.

The community witnessed firsthand how the members loved each other. We encouraged and helped those who were sick. We cried and prayed with those who grieved. We shared with those in need. In fact, the other teams in the city coed softball league would tell you that we even enjoyed simply spending time together.

The city of Casper had a favorable impression of Christ because they had a favorable impression of God's people. And every member of College Heights enjoyed the benefits of a loving, caring church community. Although not perfect, this local body of believers sought to do life together as Christ intended.

We can never experience all God has for us apart from a local body of believers. Jesus made it clear to His disciples that God designed the Christian life to be lived in the context of community.

LEARNING IT

Peter spent roughly three years learning from Jesus how to live in a community of Christ-followers. This group traveled together, ate together, and did life together. But Jesus didn't merely teach about love and service. He set the example.

Read John 13:1–17. **Why did Jesus wash the disciples' feet? (Look back at verse 1 to help you with your answer.)**

Lack of paved roads and proper footwear in the first century created perpetually dirty feet. Foot washing was a necessary but demeaning task usually reserved for the lowest, most humble servant. Although the disciples had already argued that night about which one of them was the greatest (see Luke 22:24) Jesus readily humbled Himself to demonstrate His love for them. Jesus willingly set aside His rightful place of superiority as their Master and Teacher to meet a need and set an example. The disciples' feet were dirty so Jesus washed them.

In what way did this act of love mirror Jesus' greatest act of love which He accomplished only a few hours later? (See Philippians 2:5–8 to help with your answer.)

Why do you suppose none of the disciples offered to wash the others' feet? (Check all you think apply.)

___ It never even entered their minds to serve the others in this way.

___ None of them wanted to appear inferior to the others.

___ They each thought the task was beneath them.

___ They each hoped someone else would do it.

⇥ Look back at the statements in the question above. Can you think of any task or need in your church or family about which you have one or more of these attitudes? If so, what are the needs, and your attitudes?

Jesus established a standard for all His disciples—then and now—through this humble act of service. If Jesus Christ willingly laid aside His divine rights to serve those He created, why do we, His children, sometimes have so much trouble humbly serving one another?

Read John 15:9–17. What command does Jesus give twice in this short passage?

What is the basis for this command?

This passage is so rich in spiritual truth. First, Jesus made it very clear that we cannot separate our love for Him from our love for His children. If we love Jesus we will obey Him. Jesus commanded us to love each other. Therefore, if we love Jesus we will love each other. This love is not burdensome—in fact, it brings blessings. As I love Jesus and obey Him by loving His children, I will experience the natural overflow of those relationships.

⤞ Look through John 15:9–17 again. Make a list of all the blessings you see that a Christian will experience; one who loves Jesus and obeys Him by loving other Christians.

> "And that is the higher calling to which God beckons us, a calling that transforms us from self-centered people to people focused on God and the needs of others."
>
> Kathi Macias
> *Beyond Me: Living a You-First Life in a Me-First World*

I hate to put this on paper, but I have to wonder if the reason I sometimes find it hard to love God's children as I should is because I don't love Jesus as I should. (Am I alone in this one or have you had the same trouble?) But I do want to experience the fullness of a relationship with God and His people that Jesus described in this passage.

This passage indicates we can foster our love for other Christians by reflecting on the way Jesus loves us. Spend a few moments thinking about how Jesus showed His love for you. List a few of the key ways.

In addition to the group teaching, Peter also received a little one-on-one instruction from Jesus. During a post-resurrection appearance, Jesus specifically emphasized the connection between loving Him and loving those who belong to Him. (See John 21:15–17.) Right after breakfast, on the shore of the Sea of Galilee, Jesus asked Peter three times if Peter loved Him. Three times he said, *"Yes, Lord."* And all three times Jesus replied with a command for Peter to care for His "sheep." Jesus made sure Peter got it: to love Jesus is to love and care for His body, the church.

Then a few years after Jesus' ascension, Peter benefited from the believers' love and concern for him. (See Acts 12:1–18.) King Herod was persecuting Christians. He had James put to death and Peter was awaiting a public trial after being arrested yet again.

But his brothers intervened with God on his behalf. *"So Peter was kept in prison, but the church was earnestly praying to God for him"* (Acts 12:5). God answered their prayer by sending an angel to break Peter out of jail. Then he hurried across town to Mary's house and knocked on her door while the prayer meeting was still going on!

TEACHING IT

Peter learned firsthand how Christ designed His body, the church, to function. He had both given and received the love Christ commanded. Now Peter once again faithfully taught what he had learned.

Read 1 Peter 3:8–9. **List all the characteristics and behaviors that describe how we should conduct our relationships with brothers and sisters in Christ.**

Most scholars feel that verse eight addresses our relationships with other Christians and that verse nine refers to our interaction with those outside the church. However, I have seen occasions when the truths in verse nine were needed *inside* the church as well.

⊰ Now look again at the five adjectives you listed from verse 8. Find a dictionary and locate a few synonyms for each adjective. Now write an expanded description of how Peter said we are to relate to our fellow Christians.

I don't know about you, but my life does not perfectly reflect Peter's description for brotherly behavior. In fact, some days you wouldn't recognize it in my life at all. But praise God, He is still working on me, shaping me to be the woman He wants me to be. Now, let's consider one more passage from Peter's first letter before we get serious about making some personal application.

Read 1 Peter 4:8–10. How did Peter say we should love each other and what is this kind of love capable of illustrating and being? (Note: The Greek word that is translated as "deeply" or "fervently" is an adjective that means "stretched out, continual, intense.")

Peter used the Greek word *agape* to describe the kind of love Christians should have for each other. Grammatically, verse 8 is a command. Therefore, Peter commanded his readers—including us—to love each other in a way that is benevolent and unselfish, always acting in the best interest of the other person. According to *The Expositor's Bible Commentary*, "agape love is capable of being commanded because it is not primarily an emotion but a decision of the will leading to action."

⤙ How is agape able to "cover over a multitude of sins"? (Note: Paul used this same word in 1 Corinthians 13:4–7. Read it here or in your Bible to help with your answer.)

> *Love is patient, love is kind. It does not envy, it does not boast, it is not proud. It does not dishonor others, it is not self-seeking, it is not easily angered, it keeps no record of wrongs. Love does not delight in evil, but rejoices with the truth. It always protects, always trusts, always hopes, always perseveres.*
>
> 1 Corinthians 13:4–7

In addition to the two specific examples of agape love in action that Peter gives (hospitality and service), list other ways you've seen agape in action in your own church.

LIVING IT

Jesus commanded us to love each other like He loves us. Deeply, unselfishly, with the other's best interests at heart. In this way, Jesus uses His body, the local church, to love His children. He cares for us, comforts us, provides for us, and encourages us through the hands and feet—the lives—of our brothers and sisters in Christ.

Are you committed and vitally connected to a local church body? *Read the following Scriptures that teach God's design for the church, and draw a line to connect them to the appropriate statement.*

Romans 12:5	When you were saved, you became a part of God's family.
1 Corinthians 12:18	If we belong to Christ, we also belong to each other.
Ephesians 2:19	God commands us to meet together for love and encouragement.
Hebrews 10:24–25	Love for other Christians is evidence of our salvation.
1 John 3:14	God has a place for each of us in the church.

Unshakeable Faith

⊰ Based on the passages above, describe God's will for you regarding your place in the local church.

In order to give and receive Christ's love like God commands, we must have a vita connection to a local church body. If you are not an active member of a Bible-believing local church, you are missing out on much of what God wants to give you and do through you. Please don't wait any longer to find the church where God wants you to be connected.

God has designed His church so that His children love and care for each other in reciprocal relationship. I've witnessed and benefited from many expressions of agape within the local church. But do I allow God to love others through me? How well do I meet the needs of those around me?

⊰ Prayerfully read the following Scripture passages. As you do, ask God to reveal areas in which you have failed to act with agape love toward another Christian. Write any specific response that God prompts you to make. (For example, God may prompt you to ask someone's forgiveness, meet a need, or change a behavior.)

Ephesians 4:1–3:

Ephesians 4:29–32:

Philippians 2:1–5:

Colossians 3:12–13:

1 John 3:16–18:

As we obey God's command to love others we also open our lives to be loved in the same way. As we love, we are loved in return! Hold nothing back and then get ready to see what God will do.

Read "Faith Shaker" and then answer the questions that follow.

FAITH SHAKER

Lisa's first grandchild was diagnosed with trisomy 18 during the fourth month of Anna's pregnancy. Also known as Edward's syndrome, this rare chromosomal disorder, which affects every system in the body, is usually fatal. In fact, most Trisomy 18 babies die before birth.

Anna, the oldest of Lisa's five children, and her husband, John, had been so excited to share the news that they were expecting. But the excitement soon faded. Anna's doctor ordered a sonogram and ultimately an amniocentesis after Anna experienced some bleeding late in her first trimester. The diagnosis devastated Anna, John, and both their families.

Although the tests confirmed the baby could not survive, Anna and John chose to trust God completely with the outcome. They believed her life had purpose no matter how short. They committed her to God and named her Hope Elizabeth.

Lisa wouldn't grieve in front of her family. They had always leaned on her in hard times, so she had to be strong for them. Lisa talked and prayed with them. She held them. She constantly and actively loved them.

Even though Anna and her husband lived five hours away, Lisa was a constant source of strength for them. "I had to be the strong one. Anna needed her mom. My kids and my husband depend on me and my faith."

While Lisa held up her family, God held up her. He loved her through His presence and through His people. During the months before Hope's birth, Lisa's church family prayed with her, hurt with her, and cried with her. "God sent them to cover me with love and compassion."

God also loved Lisa through His own, very real presence. "God's presence gave me a supernatural strength I can't describe. I could feel Him holding me up and sense Him whispering His comfort in my ear. His peace overwhelmed me. Even though I wept and grieved, God was there. You can't help but have faith when God shows up like that."

Hope Elizabeth was born in the 36th week of Anna's pregnancy. Hope went home to heaven sometime during labor. Lisa and her family were by their side. And many members of Lisa's church family were there too. A group from Lisa's home church made the five-hour drive to be there. They prayed with them and cried with them. Lisa and her family were overwhelmed by the love they felt.

Hope never took a breath, but her life stands as a testimony to God's love and faithfulness. Although the family still grieves their loss, Lisa says their faith was never shaken. "Our faith in God does not depend on our circumstance. Our faith isn't in an outcome. Our faith is in God."

In what ways did Lisa give God's love in the midst of grief?

How did God love and support Lisa?

In what ways did the church love Lisa?

Unshakeable Faith

Have you ever experienced the church's love and care in a similar fashion? If so, what was the circumstance?

Do you know of a need right now in your church family that needs your love in action? List some concrete ways you can show your love.

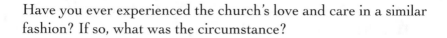

If you are a Christian, then you are a member of God's family. His purpose for you includes being vitally connected to a local church. God designed this interdependent relationship so that the members will love and serve each other in His name. Sister, if you are not experiencing this mutual relationship as an active member of a local church, please don't wait any longer to get connected. Start visiting churches and ask God to direct you to the one He has picked out for you.

As we end our last session together, prayerfully reflect on the eight faith traits we've studied.

- Secure in the God who loves and chooses you!
- Confident in your all-powerful, all-knowing, sovereign God.
- Submitted to the One who knows the future and has a plan.
- Determined to stay alert and guard against temptation.
- Lives by the power of the indwelling Holy Spirit.
- Pursues holiness with eyes focused on the Father.
- Prepared to endure persecution for the sake of Christ.
- Connected to a local church body with love and service.

How does God want you to respond to what He has taught you over the last eight weeks?

Now ask God to weave each trait into the fabric of your faith so, like Peter, you, too, can stand rock-solid in the midst of life's trials.

It's been a privilege to share Peter's faith journey with you. I pray God will continue to encourage and strengthen you through His people and through His Word.

Leader's Guide

But you are a chosen people, a royal priesthood, a holy nation,
God's special possession, that you may declare the praises of him
who called you out of darkness into his wonderful light.

—1 Peter 2:9

Thank you for your willingness to serve the women of your church by leading them through a study of *Unshakeable Faith*. I am praying God will strengthen your faith and help you stand firm through the trials of life.

Feel free to use the suggestions in this guide or adapt them as God leads. You know the needs of the women in your group. Pray before you begin each session. Ask God to apply the biblical truths found there to your life and the lives of the women in your group. Ask Him to help you lead the group in a way that fosters what He wants to do in their lives.

Don't rush as you work through each week's material. Instead, allow plenty of time for the Holy Spirit to do His job. Use a highlighter to mark questions or statements that are particularly relevant to you or your group. Try to complete the material at least a couple of days before your group meets together. That will give you time to digest what God said to you while you plan your class time.

The suggestions below are divided into three segments:

- Opening—to generate interest and introduce that session's faith trait.

- Discussion—to explore and apply that week's biblical truth.

- Wrap-up—to catch anything important missed during the discussion and, of course, to pray!

Opening

Pray to open your time together.
Use an icebreaker, special activity, or question to generate interest.
Use the following suggestions or make up your own!

WEEK ONE—choose one of the following.

- Small-group activity—Ask participants to break into groups of two or three and each share about the time they first "met" Jesus. If you have participants in your group who are not yet Christians, you can adapt or change this activity. For example: "Share with each other your impression of Jesus when you heard about Him for the first time."

- Question—Where do people often turn for acceptance, security, fulfillment, and love?

WEEK TWO—choose one of the following.

- Question—If you had the chance to be best friends with someone in the world who is rich, powerful, talented, or popular, who would it be? What kind of doors could they open for you?

- Question—Have you ever received special treatment strictly because of someone you knew? Tell us about it.

WEEK THREE

- Obstacle Course Activity—Set up a small obstacle course across your meeting room using a few chairs and other similar objects. Ask for two volunteers. Blindfold one. Ask the other volunteer to guide the blindfolded volunteer through the obstacle course using voice commands. After they have successfully completed the course, ask the group how this activity demonstrates a life of submission to God.

- Question—Why do many of us find it so difficult to submit our will to God's? Why do we continue to fight to have our own way?

Week Four

- Question—Name some measures we take to protect our possessions, selves, and family. (Some examples include home and car alarms, insurance, self-defense classes, and deadbolts.)

- Object Lesson—Bring to group several examples of ways we can lock-up or make things safe. You might bring a chain and padlock, a security lockbox, a diary with a lock and key. Ask the group to brainstorm things they could keep safe with the things you brought.

Week Five

- Object Lesson—Bring several items that need batteries to operate. You might include a flashlight, a camera, remote controlled car, and a portable CD player. Remove all the batteries before displaying them. Ask for volunteers who are willing to demonstrate the operation of one of the items. On your cue, ask them all to turn their items on together. Discuss why the items didn't work. Make the point that these items cannot serve their purpose without the proper power. If you like, finish the session by distributing the proper batteries and trying the items again.

- Question—Ask participants to name as many sources of power they can think of and some ways each is used. (For example, coal is used to produce heat, wind generates electricity, and gasoline runs our car engines.)

Week Six

- Object Lesson—Bring a small photo frame with photo, body lotion, paper towels, and glass cleaner to class. Smear the glass of the framed photo with the lotion so it is impossible to see the photo. Ask the participants to tell you something about the photo and hold it up for them to see. After they confirm that they cannot see the photo clearly enough, use the paper towels and glass cleaner to clean the lotion off the glass. Now ask them the following question.

- Question—Ask participants to share the most- and least-favorite cleaning chore.

Week Seven

- Question—How does sharing a trial or difficult experience with another person foster intimacy or deepen your relationship?
- Question—Tell us about a time you bonded with someone you didn't know well after sharing a difficult experience together.

Week Eight

- Activity—Bring several shoes with regular tie laces to class. Ask your group to break up into pairs. The object of the activity is to get the teams to work together to tie the laces. Each person is only allowed to use one hand. First ask one member only of each team to attempt to tie the shoe. It should be next to impossible with only one hand. Then allow the team partner to help. With each team member still using one hand, encourage the teams to work together to tie the shoe.

- Question—Based on what we've learned this week, explain this quote by Henry and Melvin Blackaby from their book *Experiencing God Together*. "We can claim to love God all we want, but if we are not intimately connected to the people of God, we are deceiving ourselves."

Ask for someone to read and elaborate on this week's faith trait. What is it? How can that characteristic strengthen our faith and help us stand firm in difficult times?

Group Discussion

Ask the questions marked with the discussion icon. These questions either highlight that week's faith trait, foster personal application of biblical truth, or encourage personal spiritual growth.

Include any other questions you feel best shows how Peter learned the trait, how Peter taught the trait, and how we should live out those truths in our lives.

Be sure to include the questions and points you highlighted as you completed the session. These are the questions that specifically spoke to you or seemed particularly applicable to your group.

Be flexible. Be sensitive to the Holy Spirit's leading during your group time. Listen for topics, questions, and points that reveal God is at work in that area. As long as it is productive and relevant, feel free to redirect your discussion for a while.

Ask for a volunteer to read the "Faith Shaker" story. (If time is short, skip reading the story to the group and go right to the questions about the story.)

Ask and discuss all the questions that follow the "Faith Shaker" story.

Wrap-Up

Group input—ask one or more of the following:

- Are there any questions you want to discuss that we didn't cover?

- Are there any additional insights you had you would like to share with the group?

- Are there any other comments or questions about this week's topic?

Ask the group for volunteers to share what God showed them about that week's faith trait, in relation to their own lives.

Closing prayertime—The following are a few suggestions to enrich your group's prayertime. Feel free to use the same format each week or vary it as you feel led.

- Prayer request slips—Have slips of paper available at the beginning of group time. Ask participants to write their requests. Collect the slips before the end of class in a bowl or basket. Then pass the container, and ask those who would like to participate to take one or more slips. Ask them to pray for those requests during the closing prayertime and during the week. As the leader, be prepared to pray for any requests left in the basket.

- Small-group prayer—Divide participants into groups of three or four. Ask them to share briefly their trials and needs with each other and then spend the *majority* of the allotted time in prayer together.

- Prayer partners—Assign prayer partners the first week of class to last throughout the study. These will be the groups for prayertime at the end of class. Also encourage the partners to communicate with each other during the week to share their struggles and needs.

My Faith Journey

Faith Trait One:
Secure in the God Who Loves and Chooses You

My Faith Journey

Faith Trait Two:
Confident in Your All-Powerful, All-Knowing, Sovereign God

MY FAITH JOURNEY

Faith Trait Three:
Submitted to the One Who Knows the Future and Has a Plan

_____

_____

_____

_____

_____

_____

_____

_____

_____

_____

_____

_____

_____

_____

_____

_____

_____

_____

_____

_____

_____

My Faith Journey

Faith Trait Four:
Determined to Stay Alert and Guard Against Temptation

MY FAITH JOURNEY

Faith Trait Five:
Lives by the Power of the Indwelling Holy Spirit

MY FAITH JOURNEY

Faith Trait Six:
Pursues Holiness with Eyes Focused on the Father

My Faith Journey

Faith Trait Seven:
Prepared to Endure Persecution for the Sake of Christ

My Faith Journey

Faith Trait Eight:
Connected to a Local Church Body with Love and Service